THE HIGHLAND GAMES

THE ESSENTIAL GUIDE TO

The Highland Games

MICHAEL BRANDER

CANONGATE

First published in Great Britain in 1992 by
Canongate Press plc
14 Frederick Street
EDINBURGH EH2 2HB

The publishers gratefully acknowledge permission granted from the following sources for the right to reproduce photographs in *The Essential Guide to the Highland Games:* (in order of their appearance) The Scottish Games Association; The Scottish Games Association; The Scottish Games Association; The Scottish Games Association; Stephen G. Avery; Stephen G. Avery; Fergus Highland Games and Scottish Festival; The Casket Newspaper, Antigonish; The Scottish-American Society of Central Florida, Inc.; Norman Campbell; Norman Campbell; The Casket Newspaper, Antigonish; Fergus Highland Games and Scottish Festival; Fergus Highland Games and Scottish Festival; John Paul, Inverness; The Scottish Games Association; John Paul, Inverness.

British Library Cataloguing-in-Publication Data
A catalogue record for this book is available on request from the British Library.

ISBN 0 86241 302 8
Typeset by Falcon Typographic Art Ltd, Edinburgh
Printed and bound in Great Britain by
BPCC Hazells Ltd
Member of BPCC Ltd

Contents

Preface

Highland dancing is controlled at an international level by the Scottish Official Board of Highland Dancing and Piping and pipe bands are also judged by recognised international standards. In the twenty-five Amateur Highland Games in Scotland the athletic events are judged by Olympic rules. These are under the control of the Scottish Amateur Athletic Association. The majority of the Highland Games in Scotland, however, are run under the professional aegis of the Scottish Games Association. The SGA was inaugurated in 1946 with around twenty professional Highland Games. It now controls well over fifty Highland Games in Scotland and a number of affiliated Games internationally. Clearly it is in the interests of all those involved in Highland Games anywhere around the world to be affiliated to the official governing bodies in Scotland, who are always willing to provide help and advice to organisers. The Secretary of the SGA is: Andrew Rettie, 24 Florence Place, Perth PH1 5BH *Tel*: (0738) 27782. He will be pleased to hear from any overseas Games organisers. The address of the SAAA is Caledonia House, South Gyle, Edinburgh EH12 9DQ. Canongate, the publishers of this book, will also be pleased to hear of any new Highland Games, Professional or Amateur or of details of changes in old Games, or of any that may have been overlooked, to keep further editions fully up to date. Canongate is pleased to note that both the SGA and the SAAA officially approve this *Essential Guide to the Highland Games*.

Acknowledgements

In the process of acquiring information on the very numerous Highland Games and Gatherings around the world my thanks must go to all those Highland Games Secretaries and Organisers, as well as the officers of many other associated bodies, who have been so enormously helpful and without whom this book could never have been written. That some letters have gone astray has been inevitable, since addresses are constantly changing in these matters, but I have done my best to provide as complete a coverage as possible and any Games, or points, missed, will I trust be included in any subsequent edition. Amongst the very numerous people who have been so helpful it is almost invidious to note any particular individuals; however I must take the opportunity of putting on record my debt to the following, although not necessarily in this order:

Scotland: Andrew Rettie, The Secretary, The Scottish Games Association. Gregor Nicholson, Administrator, Scottish Athletics, Edinburgh. George Spence, Convenor, Highland Games Commission. Ian Russell, The Scottish Sports Council. George Hunter, Commonwealth Games Council. Jack Richmond, Newtonmore. Alastair MacIntyre, Banavie. Roger Hutchinson, Skye. Roger Smith, The Scottish World, Oban. Australia: The Australian Tourist Commission, London. Mrs Gwen MacLennan, The Scottish Australian Heritage Council, Sydney, NSW. Mr Rod McGee, Tasmanian Pipe Band Assn. Mrs D. Laverty,

Tasmanian Caledonian Council. USA: Grace-Ellen McCrann, N American Office of the *Scottish World*. Donovan H. Bond, Editor, the *Scottish American*. Canada: The Librarian, The Canadian High Commission, Canada House, London. The Hon Jack MacIsaac, Minister of Mines and Energy, Halifax, Nova Scotia. Andy McDonald, President of the Canadian Highland Games Council, Brantford, Ontario. Angus and Marcie Macquarrie, of the *Clansman*, Halifax NS. Sr Donald A.Porter, Manitoba Highland Gathering, Selkirk. Indonesia: Jakarta, Sandy MacFarlane. New Zealand: The Librarian, The New Zealand High Commission, New Zealand House, London. Rob Shand of Fairlie, Don Fitchet of Turakina and many others, particularly my old friend Dr Randall Allardyce for collating so much information from various sources. S Africa: Alison Whitfield of Satour, The South African Tourism Board. Charles Wilson, FSA Scot, and many others, particularly numerous Tourist Boards, both at home and around the world. For any omissions, or errors, however, I am entirely responsible.

The Early Background

A Race Apart

Secluded in their straths and glens, isolated not only by the trackless mountains which encompassed them, but also by their separate language – Gaelic – the Highlanders remained a race apart, insulated from the rest of Scotland and from the advances of civilisation, until the early part of the eighteenth century. Differing from the Lowlanders radically in culture, speech and thought, the Highlanders were as unable to understand the Lowland way of life as the Lowlanders were to comprehend theirs. By 1700 the Highland style of living appeared to have changed remarkably little in essentials over the previous seven hundred years, although already the pressures of the world outside were beginning to make themselves felt.

The Clan System

In practice, of course, during the period from AD 1000 to AD 1700 there had been some gradual changes in the Highland way of life, although in general these had evolved slowly enough to be barely noticeable. Thus the original groups of comparatively small family and patriarchal units had developed into a larger and more complex social system of clans and septs, or dependents. The clan chieftain in many cases literally held the power of life or death over clan members. He had also come to be considered the superior landlord, but his powers in this respect were generally delegated through a series of leading clansmen known as Tacksmen, who sub-leased the land to individuals and family groups within the clan.

Highland Garb
The dress of the Highlanders had slowly evolved from the *leine croich*, the saffron-coloured shirt of earlier days, a kilted garment with long sleeves and pleats, to the *feileadh mor*, or belted plaid, consisting of some sixteen to eighteen feet of double-width cloth. The latter was usually worn on top of the former, or a similar type of long shirt or vest, providing an effective protection against the elements. Half of the *feileadh mor* was folded in pleats and buckled round the waist by a broad belt, forming a kilt, with the rest draped over the shoulder as a plaid to be used as a shelter from the elements if required. This multi-purpose garment also served as a blanket to sleep beneath at night. When going into battle, or when particularly physical exertion was required, the belted plaid would be cast aside. The senior members of the clan often adopted the trews, or *truis*, a type of close-fitting tartan trousers cut on the bias with the foot included, something like a pair of tartan tights. These were mostly worn when riding the small sure-footed Highland ponies, the only type of horse that could cope with the difficult terrain.

Weapons
Apart from their distinctive dress and language, the Highlanders also differed from the Lowlanders in carrying weapons as a matter of course. When fully armed they carried a targe, or circular spiked leather shield, on the left arm, and a sword attached to their belt. Latterly this would be a basket-hilted broadsword, preferably with a blade by Andrea Ferrara, reputedly the best swordsmith

in Europe. At the waist there would also be a dirk, or dagger, and concealed under the armpit a small knife, or *sgian dhu*. In the later seventeenth century they would also carry a pair of dags, or pistols, at the waist and a long-barrelled musket over their shoulder. In earlier times they were good shots with bow and arrow. Small wonder that the Highlander going to war was often accompanied by a gillie, or servant, who carried his arms for him until they were required. When attacking the enemy they would first discharge their musket, cast it aside, and then run forward within range of their dags. These would be fired in succession, then the heavy weapons would be hurled at the enemy, followed swiftly with the broadsword and targe. The combined effect must have been disconcerting to say the least to troops unaccustomed to these methods of fighting.

Music
During the sixteenth and seventeenth centuries the clarsach, the old Celtic harp which had been the principal instrument of the Highlands, gave way to the fiddle and the bagpipes. The latter, at first with just one drone then later with two, was still only the forerunner of the modern three-droned instrument. The dancing which accompanied the music of these instruments, like the mouth music of the Gaels, was of far older origin. Naturally enough, however, both music and dancing evolved over the centuries, along with the culture of the Highlanders themselves.

Usquebaugh
One important change took place during the sixteenth and seventeenth centuries, which was to have a notable effect on the Highlanders. This

was the introduction of the distillation and the making of *usquebaugh*, the Water of Life, soon shortened to uske, or usky, hence to whisky. By the start of the eighteenth century the making and drinking of whisky was a serious occupation throughout the Highlands. Twice distilled in the traditional bulbous copper pot stills, there are few drinks more suited to a climate, a country, and a people than Scotch malt whisky to the Scottish Highlanders. The very ingredients – Highland barley grown in the fertile straths, malted and dried over peat fires with perhaps some heather roots added, then mixed with the soft Highland water – were enough in themselves to justify the claim that it was the product of the Highland countryside uniquely suitable for the Highlanders who made it.

Relaxations

With or without whisky, the Highlanders were a high-spirited people – proud, yet ready to stand by any blood-related kin, however remote the relationship might be; warlike, quick to take offence; and at the same time, like most mountain dwellers, hardy and hospitable. Forced to rely on their own amusements and sports, they had a great oral tradition of poetry and story-telling. They also leaned towards activities involving feats of strength and agility suited to their outdoor life spent traversing the rocky mountainsides and crossing the swift-flowing burns and treacherous bogs. Their sports involved individuals matching themselves against others in racing, leaping, or in feats of strength and agility. In all these sports of the Gaels, music and dancing played a great part. One exception, more in keeping with their warlike nature, was one of the earliest sports recorded, involving the use of a caman, or crooked club, and a wooden ball, with two sides of roughly equal numbers vying against each other.

Pipers
Since music played such an important part in the life of the Highlanders, understandably the clan chieftain's harpist – or later his personal piper – was an important member of the clan. Not only was he the maker of music, composer alike of war marches, funeral laments and wedding dances, but he was usually also the clan historian, recording the deeds of its warriors in battle, the passing of a clan chieftain, and other important events. The piper's music was capable of inspiring the clansmen to greater exertions in battle, or in sport. Relaxing after their exertions they would dance to the music of his pipes. Songs sung in ballad-form to his music were handed down by word of mouth from generation to generation. Since inter-clan warfare was commonplace up to the seventeenth century there were thus usually two or more contradictory versions of the same event.

Tainchel
When celebrating in times of peace one of the Highlanders' favourite pastimes was the *tainchel*, or great hunt. For these very often more than one clan would combine. The chieftains would send word round to the clansmen that such a hunt was planned and where they should assemble and when. Then for several days the greater part of the clansmen thus assembled would go out into the mountains driving the red deer and other animals in front of them in a gradually tightening circle. Finally the beasts would be

driven off the mountains and through the passes, where the waiting huntsmen, armed with guns, bows and arrows and swords, and accompanied by swift deerhounds, would fall on them, killing large numbers.

The Forerunners of the Highland Games

After such a successful hunt, a great feast and celebration would be held and venison would be sent to everyone who was unable to attend. Then the rival clansmen would relax by testing each other's prowess at various sports – in running, jumping, wrestling, or primitive forms of weight putting with boulders, or divided into roughly equal sides vying against each other in a very early form of *camanachd* or shinty, with a crooked club, or caman, and a camanachd or ball formed from wood. Lastly the clansmen would vie with each other in piping and in dancing, the pipers taking it in turns to demonstrate their skills and the clansmen to demonstrate their agility and neatness of movement by dancing complicated steps to the pipe music. These relaxations were in effect the forerunners of the modern Highland Games.

Personal Combat

Such sports and activities ensured that the Highlanders kept fit for war, and their naturally hot dispositions ensured that they practised their swordplay and tested their skill and agility in wrestling with each other. Personal combat in one form or another was commonplace, but even when it came to swordplay it was seldom that anyone was killed or seriously injured, for the use of the targe and sword usually resulted in the expenditure of much energy without great damage to the person. Once blood had been drawn, honour was usually considered to be satisfied and the combatants would probably then turn to drinking or playing the pipes in perfect harmony. Only in inter-clan warfare, where there was bad blood between the two sides, were there likely to be any deaths or serious injury resulting from swordplay.

Running Across Country
In the wild and mountainous Highland country-side, where no roads existed and peat bogs, boulders and scree, or fast-flowing burns were likely to slow down, cripple or even drown the most surefooted horse, by far the quickest means of communication was by a man running across country.

Crann-tara
The *Crann-tara*, or Fiery Cross, was the age-old method of raising the clansmen in time of need. Made of two pieces of wood fastened together in the shape of a cross, the *Crann-tara* had one end alight, with a piece of linen soaked in blood attached to the other end. Runners were despatched to all points of the compass and as they ran they shouted the war cry of the clan and the place and the time chosen for a general assembly. Each clansman summoned would take up the cross afresh until all had finally been warned.

The First Braemar Gathering
From the very earliest times the clan chieftains would arrange races amongst their followers to find the fastest man available for carrying such messages in times of emergency. Legend has it that one of the first races run for the purpose of choosing the fleetest of foot as a personal envoy

was organised by Malcolm Canmore (1057–93). It is said he offered a purse of gold and a fine sword – in addition to the honour of the post – to the first runner to gain the top of Craig Choinich, one of the mountains above Braemar, and return to the starting point. A large number set off led by two Macgregor brothers, famed as the most fleet of foot in the area and firm favourites. Soon after they had started, a third and younger Macgregor brother ran forward requesting permission to join the race. Although his chances seemed hopeless, he was granted permission, and the onlookers were soon amazed to see him overtaking the others at great speed. As they approached the summit only his two brothers remained ahead of him.

'Will ye share the prize?' he demanded, as they turned downhill and he came up behind them.

'Each man for himself!' was the confident reply.

Soon he was in second place and pressing his eldest brother. As they neared the finishing point he dashed past his elder brother to take the lead. As he passed him the latter seized him despairingly by the kilt but, slipping out of it, the youngest Macgregor staggered past the post the winner.

Highland Dancing
The Highlanders were always fond of dancing and from their chieftain's viewpoint this was something to be encouraged. The lighter his men could be on their feet, the more nimble they were likely to be when crossing stony or boggy ground over which they often had to fight or travel. Lightness of foot and co-ordination of limb, which were inculcated by playing games with ball and caman, or by dancing, were important aspects of life in the Highlands as well as being a good means of relaxing pent-up spirits, which might otherwise

have found a more destructive outlet. When the Highlanders were cold dancing was a practical way of keeping warm and when they were drinking whisky the exercise helped to neutralise the potent effects of the spirit. From every viewpoint it was a satisfactory form of recreation!

The Sword Dance
It is to Malcolm Canmore again that the famed Sword Dance is generally attributed, although it is likely that it actually has much older origins. It is said that, after defeating an enemy in mortal combat, Malcolm Canmore took his vanquished opponent's sword and, laying his own across it, then proceeded to perform a dance, inventing the steps as he went along. From this impromptu dance the present Sword Dance is said to have developed.

The Stones of Strength
As well as encouraging general agility, fleetness of foot, endurance and stamina by such practices, the clan chieftains also used to measure their clansmen's strength by testing their ability to lift, or throw, certain stones, which were appropriately known as stones of strength. Such stones were generally kept close to the chieftain's castle, or some similar convenient public place. They were of two kinds, the Clach Cuid Fir, the Manhood Stone, a large stone weighing anything from a hundredweight upwards, or the Clach Neart, the Stone of Strength, which weighed only a matter of thirty pounds or so.

The Clach Cuid Fir
In the case of the Clach Cuid Fir the object was to raise the stone from the ground to chest or shoulder

level, or above the head, thereafter generally placing it on a wall or similar place. The difficulty of raising a smooth boulder from the ground is not easily understood by those who have never attempted it. Any young clansman who proved himself capable of this feat would be deemed to have attained manhood, hence the name.

The Putbrach and the Stones of Dee
Various well-known examples of Clach Cuid Fir stones may still be found in the Highlands today. At Inver, a small village close to Braemar, there is a Manhood Stone weighing 285 pounds. Another stone, named the Putbrach, is to be seen outside Balquhidder Churchyard. Two other famous stones can be found at the Bridge of Potarch; weighing together 785 pounds, they are known as the Stones of Dee.

The Clach Neart
The Clach Neart, by contrast, was generally thrown, or putted, the distance covered being the measure of this feat of strength. Here again the young man who could throw the stone a given distance was deemed to have attained manhood. On occasions one man might pit his ability against another to see who could throw the stone furthest. Such stones would generally be rounded stones from a local river bed, weighing anything from ten to thirty pounds. By this means the chieftain would be able to assess the comparative strength of his men or, for that matter, of any stranger who might visit them.

Origin of Tossing the Caber
With the growth of forestry in the Highlands, in Speyside especially, from the late sixteenth and

early seventeenth centuries onwards a fresh form of athletic skill was acquired. The Highlanders engaged in forestry work were known as floaters, since part of their task was to float the logs, once felled, down the river in rafts to the sea. An ability to pitch the logs well into the river became an essential requirement in their occupation. Tossing the *cabar*, as it is spelled in the Gaelic, or caber, as it is more generally known, became a recognised sport or pastime in the Highlands as a result.

Origin of Throwing the Hammer

Since a blacksmith's forge was to be found in almost every glen, it is not surprising that another Highland pastime was throwing the hammer. The blacksmith's hammer lying in his forge would be hurled as far as the sturdy muscles of his assistants could throw it. This too became one of the many simple sports practised in the Highlands, again making use of materials which lay to hand.

Individual and Team Sports

In general the Highlanders preferred to compete in sports where the individual could demonstrate his excellence. Hence dancing, piping, running, weight putting, hammer throwing, caber tossing, jumping and leaping would all be part of a day's programme of sport. Even in the one team game they seem to have enjoyed, the forerunner of the modern game of shinty, or *camanachd*, with its requirement for nimbleness and endurance, the emphasis was on the individual rather than the team. Thus when rival clans met after a *tainchel* or on a similar occasion, the contests were in the main between individuals rather than rival teams. Each clan's champions would compete in running, leaping, putting the weight or stone and in tossing the caber; their rival musicians, pipers, and fiddlers would compete against each other and the clansmen would soon be displaying their skills at dancing, rivalling each other in yet another field.

Origins of the Modern Games

It must be appreciated that the Highland sports were always tests not only of strength and muscle power, but also of character. Considerable skill and practice were needed to excel, so that sheer size and weight did not necessarily win the day. Co-ordination and agility were required above all. Musical ability and fitness were also essential attributes in Highland dancing and piping, which were an integral part of the Highland way of life. It was from these beginnings, seeking relief from the harsh conditions of clan life in the Highlands, that the modern Highland Games have gradually developed over the centuries.

From the Eighteenth to the Twentieth Century

A Time of Change in the Highlands

During the eighteenth century the Highlands saw the gradual break-up of the clan system and the dispersal of the Highlanders themselves. The sensational series of victories by Montrose in his brief but whirlwind campaign of 1644–45, which he started by sending the Fiery Cross around the Highlands, had made the Highlanders both loathed and feared in the Lowlands of Scotland. The Union of the Parliaments in 1707 was followed by the Rebellion of 1715 when the Earl of Mar raised the Royal Standard at Braemar and the Old Pretender signally failed to raise the nation. The resulting repressive measures in the Highlands, such as the so-called Disarming Acts, were more honoured in the breach than in the observance. In the 1720s, however, General Wade began to implement his plan to build roads across the Highlands, linking a series of forts. By 1723 he had built over 250 miles of roads and forty bridges connecting Fort William, Fort Augustus and Fort George and extending from Crieff to Inverness. Although used more by the rebels than the government forces during the 1745 Rebellion, they were to be utilised subsequently in maintaining the repressive rule which followed Culloden.

After Culloden

It has been suggested that the first massed pipe bands were heard when the Jacobite Highlanders flocked to Prince Charles Edward Stuart's banner at Glenfinnan and afterwards on his triumphal march southwards. There may be an element of truth in this, but there were few pipes to be heard beyond those in the Highland regiments when the Duke of Cumberland had taken his bloody revenge after his victory at Culloden. Apart from the general harrying of the Highlands, the kilt, tartans, and pipes were all proscribed, as was the carrying of arms, and this time the Disarming Acts were savagely enforced. The power of the chieftains was greatly curtailed by the new laws, and the old clan way of life virtually came to an end, although, like any well-rooted institution, it was a long time a-dying.

People Versus Sheep

The latter half of the eighteenth century and the first half of the nineteenth saw most of the old ways of the Highlands changing fast. The chieftains were demoted by the new laws into mere landlords, and their clansmen found themselves relegated to the status of tenants. No longer required to answer a call to arms at a moment's notice the clansmen became instead poor relations providing little useful return. Cattle proved a much better investment, yielding a substantial and visible profit. When the chieftains found in the last quarter of the eighteenth century that sheep gave an even better and quicker financial profit, their tenantry became no more than a burden, using up land which was capable of providing a far better income under sheep. It was then that the infamous Clearances began.

Highland Dress Restored

Despite the repression which followed the 1745 Rising, the worst was over by the end of the first decade. The Highland regiments soon won such widespread esteem throughout Britain, and their deeds were so often lauded by the Press and all who saw them in action, that there was a very considerable easing of the restrictions. Two decades later, in 1778, the Highland Society of London was formed by exiled Highlanders in the capital. They were instrumental in lobbying for the repeal of the Act against Highland Dress, which had clearly outlived its time. In 1782 the Act was duly repealed and it is clear what the kilt and the tartans still meant to the Highlanders from the tone of the following proclamation which was posted, in Gaelic, throughout the Highlands:

Listen Men!
This is bringing before all the sons of Gael that the King and Parliament of Britain have for ever abolished the Act against the Highland Dress that came down to the Clans from the beginning of the world to 1746. This must bring great joy to every Highland heart. You are no longer bound down to the unmanly dress of the Lowlanders. This is declaring to every man, young and old, simple and gentle, that they may after this put on and wear the trews, the little kilt, the doublet and hose, along with the tartan kilt, without fear of the law of the land or the spite of enemies.

Introduction of the Feileadh Beg
The old *feileadh mor*, or belted plaid, was inconvenient to wear, as it tended to cramp the use of the arm over which the plaid was flung. At some time during the mid-eighteenth century it gave way to the *feileadh beg*, or little kilt, much as it is worn today. Whether, as has been maintained, this was

invented in Glengarry by an English ironmaster named Rawlinson, with the aid of an English tailor named Parkinson, is completely by the way. The convenience of the 'philibeg', or little kilt, was immediately apparent and it was clearly a sensible and useful adaptation of the older and more cumbersome style of dress. Both in work and in relaxation, in peace and in war, it was a considerable improvement on the old garb. It would, for instance, have been virtually impossible to toss the caber wearing the old *feileadh mor*. It would have had to be discarded in the same way that it was always cast aside by the Highlanders just before they charged the enemy, to be left lying on the battlefield and recovered later.

Highlanders' Attitude to Trousers

Judging from the notice quoted above it will be appreciated how strongly the Highlanders disliked the Lowland dress they had been forced to wear. To them trousers were an unmanly, cumbersome, and uncomfortable garment. To those used to fording Highland burns thigh deep during the course of a day's journey, there was no comparison between the convenience and comfort of the two, since the kilt was soon dry whereas the trousers remained soaking wet all day.

Shean Triubhs

One of the better known Highland dances, commonly performed at the Highland Games, is known as the *Shean Triubhs*, which is the Gaelic for 'old trousers'. It is said that the shaking movements of the leg during this dance are meant to symbolise the shaking-off of the hated trousers, but this is unlikely since the trews were common enough wear prior to the 1745 and in any event the dance

26

dates from a good deal earlier. It may, however, be that the dance was used to make a mockery of the hated southern dress, for if the Lowlander feared and hated the Highlanders, the dislike was returned in full measure, in both cases extending to their customary garb.

The Highland Society of London

In addition to their major success in having the ban on Highland dress lifted, the Highland Society of London, for the most part composed of wealthy and influential young exiles, also encouraged general standards of piping. To this end they instituted an annual competition for a gold medal. They also encouraged Highland dancing and the wearing of Highland dress. As so often the case, it was the Scots outside Scotland itself who proved most enthusiastic about matters Scottish! It is an interesting national characteristic that there is never a more vociferous enthusiast for Scotland and all things Scottish than the expatriate Scot, forced to leave his native land through the exigencies of Fate and the necessity to earn money elsewhere. This national characteristic does not seem to diminish very greatly even after several generations of exile. Hence the fact that pipe bands and Highland Games are to be found flourishing in many parts of the USA and elsewhere around the world, with the grandsons, great-grandsons, and even more distant kin of expatriate Scots proudly wearing the kilt and taking their part in the proceedings.

Early Highland Gatherings

The first Highland Society Gathering was held in 1781 at the Falkirk Tryst, this being where the Highland cattle were gathered together to be sold prior to despatch to England. Nineteen

years later in 1800 three Braemar carpenters, or
wheelwrights, formed a Friendly Society, whose
activities included an annual 'Wright's Walk' wearing full Highland dress; from these humble beginnings was to emerge the famous annual Braemar
Gathering. In 1817, after the return of so many
Highland soldiers from the wars, the first full-
scale Braemar Gathering evolved. By 1819 the St
Fillan's Society was also promoting annual Highland Games, which included the Sword Dance,
hitherto thought too warlike to be allowed. From
this stage onwards the Highland Games grew in
popularity throughout the Highlands. Ceres in
Fife regards its Highland Games as the oldest,
claiming to have had an annual Games since its
men returned from Bannockburn in 1314. Certainly
all the Highland Games owe much to the military
training of the Highlanders for it was undoubtedly
during army service that many aspects of the
Highland Games were developed and improved.

Formation of the Highland Regiments

During the period from 1740 to 1815 some eighty-
six Highland regiments were formed, including
the militia regiments. After Culloden, the Highland
regiments were the only place the Highlanders
were entitled to wear the kilt and carry arms
without interference. The war in Europe and in
North America against France soon produced an
almost never-ending need for fighting men. The
government in the south was happy to enlist as
many Highlanders as cared to join the army. With
the outbreak of the American War of Independ-
ence more soldiers were required, then came
the Napoleonic Wars. Many of the newly formed
Highland regiments were sent abroad and as many
were killed by disease and the effects of foreign

climates as by enemy action. Yet others did not return because they were offered land abroad and saw a better future there than returning to the Highlands where their families had been evicted and their homes burned to make way for sheep in the notorious Clearances.

Regimental Games

Regarding themselves as an extension of the family or clan, the Highland regiments followed many of the old clan principles. Most of the old Highland sports were perpetuated by the soldiers. Piping and dancing in particular were practised wherever they might be, simply as a natural form of relaxation, and as time passed became formally organised in the way of all army pursuits. Competition between the Highland regiments was also encouraged, and whenever the opportunity arose a version of their native Highland Games might be arranged. Thus weight putting, leaping, jumping and running were all seen as regimental, or interregimental, sports to be practised as the occasion arose. *Camanachd*, or the game of shinty, might also be played where sufficient camans, or bent sticks, could be found. The commanding officers of the Highland regiments, like the chieftains of old, saw the advantages of encouraging sports and pastimes which kept their men fit, agile, and strong.

Emigration

By the end of the Napoleonic Wars the Highlanders were gradually being squeezed out of the Highlands. The Sutherland Clearances of 1819 at Strathnaver followed the earlier Clearances at Kildonan. In each case several thousand ablebodied tenants were evicted from townships they had occupied since time immemorial to make way for sheep. The brutality of the actions and the methods used caused widespread protest, but the Highlanders were nevertheless evicted. Many went abroad, feeling that there was little left worth staying for in their native land. With them they took their native language and Gaelic culture, including their Highland Games. Thus the Highland traditions continued to flourish in far-flung parts of the world, often with interesting local variants introduced by the Highlanders in their new surroundings.

George IV's Visit

In 1822 George IV visited Edinburgh, the first visit to Scotland of any British monarch since Charles II, after a gap of over 170 years. The whole affair was stage-managed by that master of illusion, Sir Walter Scott. At his instigation the corpulent and corseted King wore the full dress of a Highland chieftain, with the addition of pink silk tights for modesty's sake. His kilt was somewhat short and one Edinburgh matron was heard to remark tartly that, 'As his visit was such a brief one it was kind of his Majesty to show so much of himself to his loyal subjects.'

The Tartan Revival

The royal visit and the growing popularity of the works of Sir Walter Scott combined to bring the tartans back into fashion at the very time some of the Highland regiments themselves had begun agitating to get rid of the kilt. Between 1822 and 1850 no fewer than six books were written about the clans and their tartans, helping to encourage a romantic view of the Highlands among visitors to Scotland. In fact many of the so-called tartans 'rescued' from oblivion were invented at this time.

Continued Clearances

Once a source of fear in the south, the Highlanders had become a symbol of fearlessness in war following the feats of the Highland regiments in many foreign fields of action during the eighteenth century. With George IV's adoption of the kilt and Sir Walter Scott's magical literary gloss, it might have seemed as if the Highlanders' future was assured. Unfortunately this was far from the case, as the continuing Clearances proved only too plainly. In the first half of the nineteenth century the evictions continued apace as sheep replaced men and left vast unpopulated spaces with only a few shepherds remaining. Understandably enough at this time the game of shinty, which had generally been played between rival townships, went into decline, but conversely there was a considerable upsurge of interest in Highland dancing in the south.

The Chieftains' Role

The landlords responsible for evicting their tenants at this time were for the most part those very men who had previously been exalted as the clan chieftains. Ironically, having failed to look after their clansmen's interests and unable to adapt to a changing world, before long many of them were forced to sell their estates and leave their native land. Macdonnell of Glengarry is a classic example. The new landlords who replaced them were in almost every case southerners, either Lowlanders or Englishmen. It is not altogether surprising that during the 1830s and 1840s there was something of an outcry against the kilt in some of the remaining Highland regiments, many now officered by southerners who did not themselves wear the kilt.

Victoria and Albert

It was the arrival of Queen Victoria as a young bride, with her German husband Prince Albert, that changed matters dramatically. On her first visit north of the Border she fell in love with everything Highland – the countryside, the tartans, the kilt, the people. In 1842 she bought the estate of Balmoral near Braemar and in the next half of the century came the Balmoralisation of the Highlands. Everything connected with the Highlands became the height of fashion – the kilt, the clan tartans (mostly newly invented), Highland dancing, the pipes and, inevitably, the Highland Games.

Popularisation of the Highlands

This was not, of course, an immediate process. It took several decades before the effects were fully visible, but the example set by the royal couple was followed faithfully by thousands of loyal southern subjects from the Lowlands of Scotland down to Bournemouth and the south coast. The royal way of life in the Highlands, the adoption of the kilt by Prince Albert, clan tartans and the whole Highland way of life were slavishly imitated. Throughout the Highlands shooting and fishing lodges were erected, with a profusion of pepperpot towers, crow-stepped gables and other features regarded as peculiarly Scottish. Their interiors were draped with varied tartans. Spears, claymores, targes, ancient arms and armour were hung on the walls and the new English landlords regarded themselves as suitably housed. Wearing the kilt and stalking the red deer or fishing for salmon, they considered themselves entirely part of the local scene. From the middle of the century onwards, when the development of the railways facilitated travel, Scotland, and the Highlands in particular, increasingly became a tourist attraction. Prominent among the attractions were the Highland Games.

Royal Presence at Braemar
In 1843 the seal of royal approval was set on the Highland Games when the royal family first attended the Braemar Gathering from nearby Balmoral. Thereafter they attended the Gathering each year. Indeed there has been scarcely a year without royal attendance since then, and this has become a recognised feature of the event. The royal example was naturally once again followed widely elsewhere, and many small and large Highland Games were revived and organised throughout the Highlands.

Victorian Rigidity
The rigidity which was so much a part of the Victorian era had its effects on most aspects of life and proved a noticeable influence on Highland dress. Thus the *sgian dhu*, the simple small knife of the past, became a bulky affair carried in the hose below the knee with a thistle handle crowned with a large cairngorm or similar jewel. The sporran became a hairy appendage covering the front of the kilt and extending to the knees. The shoes were invariably black brogues, worn frequently with lacing halfway up the leg and with holes intended to simulate those worn by the Highlanders of old, when shod at all, to allow the water to drain quickly from them after wading a burn. The jacket was cuffed and epauletted in the manner of the eighteenth-century military coat. Thus the Highlander was in danger of becoming as rigidly stereotyped as a music-hall figure, but

the sad truth was that the real Highlander by this time barely existed. The Gaelic language itself had almost disappeared with the arrival of the new breed of southern absentee landlord who worked on the well-established principle that if you simply shouted loudly enough at the natives in English they would understand in the end.

Highland Games

It was less easy for the Victorians to regularise the rules of the Highland Games. To begin with, there were few rigidly minded competitors or organisers amongst the native Scots. The spectators, who might have organised matters differently, merely saw the Highland Games as a 'romantic survival', part of the 'Noble Highlander' illusion, on a par with village pageants, clog dancing or Morris dancers, and better left alone. The truth probably was that no southern mind could conceive any way of regulating such things as tossing the caber!

Contemporary Descriptions

The Games and their lack of rigid standards were variously described by late Victorian writers. *The Encyclopedia of Sport*, published in 1897, tucked a brief entry entitled 'Highland Gatherings and Games' between larger entries for 'The Heron' and 'The Hippopotamus'. The author, E. Lennox Peel, took a very condescending view of the proceedings at the Games:

> Highland Games are often held in the midst of the most romantic scenery, and offer a very pretty contrast to the sombre and business-like surroundings of a town athletic meeting. What matter if the running path in the North

is only a moderately level grass-grown spot of irregular shape, with sudden acute-angled corners that would fill the heart of an Oxford or Cambridge president with a sense of the liveliest dismay? One such is at Glenisla, held under the shadow of Mount Blair, 2,400 feet high, with the river Isla meandering in front, where the 'going' is indifferent and where a mile in 5 minutes 5 seconds is a really fast time . . .

J. W. McCombie Smith was better informed. In his book *The Athletes and Athletic Sports of Scotland* (1892) he noted with interest that the standard weights for putting the stone were sixteen and twenty-two pounds, while the hop or run was generally limited to seven feet six inches, although the ground varied from flattish to 'indifferently level', which may be interpreted as either up- or down-hill. He also noted considerable variations in the stones used: 'a smooth round stone at Inverness, a rough-surfaced iron ball at Luss, and a lead ball with indentations for the fingers at Aboyne'.

Variety of Performance
As Lennox Peel pointed out, there was 'a wide field for variety of performance'. Three different kinds of putting were practised, for instance – the Ordinary, the Braemar and the Borders styles. Nor was this variety of performance restricted to putting alone. The caber too was likely to come in different lengths and weights. In some places it was the custom, as it still is at one or two Games, to saw a piece of the caber off by degrees until the first entrant was able to toss it. The flatness of the ground, of course, varied considerably from one Games or Gathering to the next. Even today, when

judging is much stricter and more even in the various Games than perhaps it used to be, there is bound, by the nature of things, to be a good deal of local difference between one Games and the next. This is quite aside from such imponderables as the weather. Clearly, even allowing for differences in the ground itself, if there is a howling gale blowing into the competitors' faces, or it is sleeting heavily, then performances can hardly be compared with those on a fine sunny day. There always has been a certain happy inconclusiveness about results in the various Highland Games, largely dependent on where and indeed when they are held.

Donald Dinnie

Nevertheless from 1856 to 1876, with the exception of one year when he was away in North America, the Highland Games were dominated by one man, Donald Dinnie, an erstwhile stonemason from Aberdeenshire, born at Balnacraig in 1837. Weighing fifteen stone, but described as having not an ounce of superfluous flesh on him, and standing six feet one inch in height, Dinnie must have been a formidable athlete and the records he set in various events in the Highland Games in which he competed stood for many years after his death.

Early Records

One of Dinnie's remarkable exhibitions of strength was to lift both the Stones of Dee at the Bridge of Potarch and carry them for several yards. Since the stones together weigh a matter of 785 pounds, this is a feat which has not yet been equalled, although the stones have since been lifted by at least two modern weight lifters. Merely to lift them is a feat well beyond the scope of most athletes today, even those practised in weight lifting, and it must be remembered that Dinnie was an all-rounder, equally at home putting the weight, tossing the caber, leaping, jumping or running, or for that matter Highland dancing. At high jumping Dinnie was credited with clearing five feet eleven inches. At Coupar Angus he threw a hammer of eighteen pounds, although with reputedly a very long handle, a matter of 132 feet eight inches. He putt the twenty-two-pound weight forty-two feet three inches at Dunkeld, and the sixteen-pound stone forty-nine feet six inches at Perth in 1868. These were all outstanding feats by any standards and it is small wonder that his records stood unequalled for many years.

The First World Tour
Dinnie appears to have been the first competitor to tour the world and compete in other Highland Games overseas. Apart from North America, he also visited Australia and New Zealand, as well as South Africa. In addition to giving exhibitions of his skill in putting the shot, tossing the caber, and throwing the hammer, he also competed against the local champions and gave exhibitions of Highland dancing. By the mid-nineteenth century, the Highlanders had emigrated all round the world and the Highland Games had become an internationally known feature of the Highland way of life, a well-known and colourful spectacle which was greatly appreciated.

The Highlander Abroad
With the emigration of so many Highlanders during the eighteenth and nineteenth centuries, the distinctive Highland songs, customs, and Games had all been taken abroad. In the United States of

America – notably in North Carolina – in Canada, Australia and New Zealand, Scottish emigrants established entirely Scottish enclaves where the Highland way of life continued very much as it had done in Scotland. In many cases the Gaelic language itself survived for generations, and in some instances still survives to this day.

Influence of the Highland Regiments
Wherever the Highland regiments were sent on overseas postings to remote corners of the British Empire they also took with them their Highland Games and *camanachd*. Their example and influence inevitably helped to spread an interest in the Games. In Canada, Australia, and New Zealand an interest in piping, dancing, and the usual heavy events was stimulated by the presence of Highland regiments close to the settlements of exiled Scots. Watching the Highlanders perform, the local people were often inspired to emulate the exhibitions of such agility and strength and in India and the Far East local leaders often encouraged similar activities amongst the native population.

Highland Traditions Abroad
Thus while the Highland way of life was steadily being eroded in Scotland during the eighteenth and nineteenth centuries, the Highlander abroad, whether emigrant or soldier, was instrumental in transplanting the Gaelic culture, the traditional songs, dances, pipe tunes, and familiar sports such as putting the stone, throwing the hammer or the weight, and caber tossing, as well as *camanachd*, to new lands overseas. There they can still be found flourishing, along with the kilt, the clan tartans, and clan associations, making up a worldwide heritage of which all who can claim

Scots blood may be justly proud, whether at home or overseas. It is summed up evocatively in the words of 'The Canadian Boat Song', written by an anonymous exile:

> From the lone shieling of the misty island
> Mountains divide us and a waste of seas –
> Yet still the blood is strong, the heart is
>   Highland,
> And we in dreams behold the Hebrides.

The Present Day

Development of the Games in Scotland
From the mid-nineteenth century onwards small local Highland Games proliferated throughout the Highlands, with a gradual spread southward. Games were established in places as far south as Stranraer in Galloway and as far north as Caithness and the Outer Isles. Wherever the Games were held, the heavy events, putting the stone, throwing the weight and the hammer, and tossing the caber, as well as Highland dancing and piping, were always an essential part of the proceedings. The standards of performance, as well as the other events included, varied as much as the setting, and in the same way that village cricket in England varied from pitch to pitch and village to village, so the Highland Games developed a highly individual flavour in each locality where they were held, a distinctive flavour which they retain to this day.

Individual Flavour
So much depends on the shape and size of the ground available. Not all are level by any means, and this can lend a special interest to some of the events and on occasion may favour local competitors who know the ground and can use it to their advantage. In some cases the Games organisers deliberately insist on classes restricted to locals only, while the well-known professionals with their undoubted crowd-drawing appeal may only enter the classes open to all-comers, thus

giving a chance to the local competitors to show their form. Such classes can produce some excellent performances and much keen competition.

Local Loyalties

There is also, of course, a fierce local loyalty involved in the Games and the local champion will have a strong following, although some of the well-known national champions will also have their own loyal supporters who follow their successes from Games to Games. Even at the larger and better-known Gatherings there is still likely to be a great deal of local interest. The long-distance race, for instance, may be round a special vantage point, or there may be some favourite local contest, such as tossing the sheaf, which has its own local expert exponents able to beat all-comers including the professional heavyweight champions. Or it may be that there is a special local team who are favoured in the tug-of-war, or some other contest where a local entry has a chance of winning even though competing against national champions.

Local Variations

Apart from the events normally associated with any Highland Games, or Gathering, there is often an essentially local flavour about the smaller Highland Games which adds a special piquancy to them. Thus there may be a tent with a local produce competition, adding something of the flavour of a horticultural show or Women's Rural Institute meeting to the proceedings. There may be such unusual items as a clay pigeon or rifle shooting competition, or pony trotting, or cycle racing. There is likely to be something for everyone at these local Highland Games and in this lies a great deal of their charm. They are not only a splendid spectacle, but they are also essentially a local holiday and high day, when the kilt that has been carefully preserved in mothballs for the greater part of the year is taken out and donned for the day by contestants and spectators alike. It is a day to be enjoyed and savoured and talked about for much of the year until the time comes to get down to planning the next year's events.

Heavyweight Champions

Since Donald Dinnie's long reign as heavyweight champion of the Games, there have generally been certain prominent heavyweight champions who have dominated the Highland Games circuit for a time. During the 1880s G.H. Johnstone retained the title for a decade; from 1903 to 1914 A.A. Cameron reigned supreme and from 1928 to the mid-thirties the championship was shared regularly between Ed Anderson and George Clark. Thereafter there were few individual champions over any lengthy period until after the 1939–45 war when Bill Anderson won the championship every year from 1959 to 1962. The Olympic athlete and Yorkshire-born sportsman Arthur Rowe wrested it from Anderson in 1963. From then on, for more than a decade, these two doughty rivals vied with each other for the championship, even, in 1964 and 1969, sharing it between them. Finally during the 1970s Bill Anderson went on to reign supreme, winning it from 1972 to 1978 and again in 1980, thus achieving a notable fourteen wins with two shared, against Rowe's four wins and two shared.

Dinnie and Anderson

Had it not been for Arthur Rowe's challenge, Bill Anderson might well have surpassed Donald

Dinnie's remarkable record of nineteen championships. Both Anderson and Dinnie were undoubtedly outstanding athletes and there are some
remarkable similarities between them, even though
they were separated by a gap of exactly one
hundred years. Dinnie was born in 1837 and
Anderson in 1937, both in Aberdeenshire. Both
were members of large families: Dinnie had six
brothers and four sisters, Anderson nine brothers
and two sisters. Both left school at fifteen. Dinnie
became a stonemason like his father and Anderson
a farmer like his. Dinnie turned professional at
sixteen, Anderson at seventeen. Dinnie at six feet
one inch was an inch shorter than Anderson, but
at fifteen stones without an ounce of superfluous
flesh some five stones lighter.

The 1980s
During the 1980s the Highland Games in Scotland
saw an influx of heavyweight competitors on an
international scale. In 1981 John McArdle from
Oregon made his mark. In 1982 Grant Anderson
of Dundee defeated the much feared Geoff Capes,
billed as 'the strongest man in the world', although
he was to be successful the following year. In 1985
a Dutchman Simon Wulfe and Capes tied and
thereafter Capes was again successful, although
subsequently competitors such as Chris Okonkwo
from Nigeria, Dave Harrington from Canada and
Colin Mathieson from Australia were making their
mark. This is now truly an international sport.

Professional and Amateur
In 1946 the Scottish Games Association was
inaugurated and by 1947 twenty Professional Highland Games were affiliated. Since then the number
of Highland Games under the aegis of the SGA has

nearly trebled, and this does not include the growing number of Overseas Games affiliated to them. Under the SGA rules it is possible to hold an event restricted to local entrants and a similar event open to all-comers, which prevents outsiders scooping all the prizes and encourages local competitors. There are by contrast only twenty-five Amateur Games run under Olympic Rules by the Scottish Amateur Athletic Association. These, of course, often attract a high standard of athlete, particularly in the light events, although the standard in the heavy events may not be so high. Local hill races can often be a particular attraction to competitors from far afield in the Amateur Games. Pipe band competitions are another feature which attracts both competitors and spectators to the Amateur Games. In the main, however, the following remarks relate chiefly to the Professional Games.

THE HEAVY EVENTS

Putting the Stone
Normally the heavy events start with putting the stone, traditionally a stone from the local river. A seven-foot-six-inch space is allowed for the throw, which is made from behind a four-foot-six-inch wooden marker, which is six inches high. The throw is measured from the landing mark made when the stone hits the ground. The stones may vary from around thirteen pounds to as much as twenty-eight pounds so that the distances thrown may vary enormously from one Games to the next. It is thus virtually impossible to make any real comparisons for record purposes between the various Highland Games.

Throwing the Hammer
The second event in the programme is usually

throwing the hammer, which consists of a round head and a wooden shaft, unlike the wire used in the Olympic events. No turning is allowed and the thrower grasps the handle then swings the hammer three or four times round his head before releasing it behind him. A misthrow sideways is not uncommon and in small fields this can be a hazard for spectators and judges, even though the hammer shaft is usually well covered in resin to provide a good grip.

Throwing the Weight for Distance
Throwing the weight for distance is done with a ball and chain not more than eighteen inches long with a handle attached. The two standard weights are twenty-eight pounds and, less often, fifty-six pounds. The thrower must use only one hand and has nine feet behind the marker to make three full turns before releasing the handle and hurling the weight forward. Competitors are disqualified if they unbalance themselves when throwing, and step or fall over the marker. When properly executed, this is decidedly the most graceful and eyecatching of all the heavy events, appearing deceptively simple, but in fact requiring a great deal of practice and skill to make a good throw.

Throwing the Weight Over the Bar
The weight of fifty-six pounds may be either a simple agricultural weight with a ring attached to it or a round ball with a chain of up to eighteen inches with a ring at the end. As with the high jump, the bar is raised between two posts and each entrant has three throws at each height as the bar is raised. The competitors take their stance under the bar, swing the weight one-handed between their legs

and then throw it over their heads and over the bar. Elimination results from failure to clear the bar, and heights of over fifteen feet are regularly achieved. In his delightful book, *The Games*, Charlie Allan, world champion caber-tosser in 1972 and 1973 and Scottish champion in 1974, compared it with a grown man heaving a seven-year-old child over a double-decker bus! Again, like most of the heavy event feats it looks very simple when performed by an expert, but most people would find it difficult enough to throw the weight over their heads, let alone over the bar, and it is easy enough for a competitor to endanger the spectators, or himself, with a badly managed throw.

Tossing the Caber

The event most firmly associated with the Highland Games is, of course, the caber tossing. The length and weight of the caber varies greatly, but the average caber probably weighs around 150 pounds and is about eighteen feet long, tapering from around nine or ten inches to about half that at the other end. The caber is set up by the officials with the thinner end on the ground. The competitor then bends down and takes the weight on his shoulder, clasping his hands round the lower end. Lifting it off the ground, he hitches it into the air with a slight heave and slips his hands underneath it. He then runs forward at his best speed and, halting abruptly, hurls the end he is holding as high into the air as he can. The object is to make the caber land on the heavy end so that the light end makes a perfect turn over it and lands pointing directly in line away from the thrower. Any deviation from the straight line is penalised and the best straight thrower is the winner. In some Games if no one can toss the caber, a piece is sawn off the end until it can be thrown.

Unexpected Projectiles
Getting the caber balanced initially can be a somewhat tricky moment. It is not uncommon to see the caber lifted and then start to waver slightly. If the would-be tosser cannot control this he may be forced to take a sideways step, and this can result in the caber taking charge and officials scattering wildly as the caber wavers to and fro before falling sideways! As may be imagined, a high wind can have a considerable effect on the caber and make it very difficult to control. Such incidents, of course, may generally be regarded as simply adding to the spectators' enjoyment, but it is not always a laughing matter. In most of the heavy events the officials and, indeed, in some of the smaller games, the spectators, have to keep a wary eye on the proceedings and be ready to move nimbly out of the way of unexpected projectiles. This is especially the case with throwing the hammer for distance and during the past two years several near-fatal misses have been reported. At many Games a protective net is now erected to prevent a stray hammer going off in the wrong direction. Anyone judging in the ring will agree this is a wise precaution.

THE LIGHT EVENTS

Running
The running is mainly conducted under the rules of 'Pedestrianism' as practised in the Borders and the North of England; hence, strictly speaking, it is not in the Highland tradition. The races often involve a considerable amount of gambling and

although the standards can be extremely high the times achieved are not necessarily impressive. The reason for this is simply that the competitors will only run as fast as is required to win, since they are running for money and too much effort needlessly expended in one race may cost them their due rewards in another. To some extent the same principle applies in the heavy events too, where undue straining to win in one event might affect the results in another. In the Amateur Games, of course, the competitors are all striving to achieve their best and the competition can thus be remarkably keen even if sometimes the results may not be quite so impressive as those produced by the professionals.

Jumping

The jumping events include the high jump, long jump, hop, step and jump and the pole vault, although the pole vault is becoming much less common. It is customary for competitors to enter all the events. A sandpit or inflated landing area is provided for the high jump and pole vault. Only ordinary metal poles are allowed and there is no box, or trap, provided in which to place the pole for the vault. There are, however, special spikes in the end of the pole to give a firm grip on the grass. In the hop, step and jump and the long jump there are no special run-ups or take-off boards and the take-off point of each competitor is noted by the judge.

All-Round Competitors

The competitors in the jumping usually also take part in the running or in the heavy events. Surprisingly, the competitors in the heavy events frequently prove extremely agile in the high jumping and pole vaulting. On occasion they do not have time to change from the kilt into shorts and even so have been known to perform remarkably well. Pole vaults of over ten feet and high jumps of over five feet six inches are not unknown. Considering the size of the competitors these results are highly creditable in any circumstances, let alone when wearing the kilt!

Wrestling: Cumberland Style

Another event in which the heavy competitors also usually prove able participants is the wrestling. This is generally 'Cumberland Style' wrestling, which is usually conducted with the contestants wearing the kilt. The opponents face each other chest to chest with each man placing his right arm over the other's left and grasping him round the body with his chin on the other's shoulder. Once each has his grip firmly secured, the judge gives the command 'Hold!' and the bout begins. The object is to throw, trip, or squeeze the other so that he either breaks his grip, or touches the ground with a part of the body other than his feet. There is a great deal more skill involved in this type of wrestling than would appear at first sight. In general, however, the larger and heavier the participant the better his chances. This is not to say that a skilful and well-built light-weight cannot prove unexpectedly successful against heavier but less skilled opponents.

Wrestling: Catch-As-Catch-Can

In some Highland Games an alternative type of wrestling is allowed, namely 'Catch-As-Catch-Can'. The object here is to pin the opponent's shoulders flat on the ground for three seconds. Under the Scottish Games Association rules, 'the hair, flesh, ears, private parts, or clothes, must not be seized, the twisting of fingers is forbidden and any grip that has as its object the punishing of the opponent or inflicting such pain as might cause him to give a fall will not be allowed'. Each bout in this form of wrestling lasts for ten minutes if no fall occurs and the referee then nominates a winner.

Tug-of-War
Another very popular heavy event, in this case a team contest, is the tug-of-war. Each team consists of eight men and a coach, who encourages them to pull as and when required and organises the team's effort so as to defeat their rivals. The object is to pull with nearly straight arms and legs from as low a position as possible, with all eight men working in unison. The length of the pull may vary but officially should be twelve feet. This is measured by two markers on the rope each six feet from the centre. When either mark passes the stick marking the central point the other side has won. The judges will generally start the competition with the command 'Pick up the rope!' Thereupon the two teams move back until the rope is taut and the judge then inserts the marker flag opposite the central marker on the rope. The teams thump their feet into the ground and lean back and the judge gives the command 'Pull!' whereupon the struggle of the giants begins. This is where teamwork and practice pay handsomely and a well-practised team with a good coach will almost invariably beat less efficient teamwork by a heavier team.

Grand March Past
Many Highland Games, particularly in the USA, open with a grand march past of the assembled clansmen, as for instance at Lonach, or with

the massed pipe bands. The latter can only be expected where there are pipe band competitions. Such march pasts are usually led by the chieftain of the Games and constitute a considerable spectacle. At some Games, such as Galashiels, this is combined with a Border Riding, which, although a Borders tradition rather than Highland, is also a very considerable attraction to the spectators.

Judging the Pipe Band Competitions

In pipe band competitions each band in turn is expected to play a selection of tunes lasting for some five to seven minutes. They are judged by three separate judges. The Piping Judge marks the band out of seventy-five marks; the Drumming Judge out of twenty-five marks and the third judge, a somewhat controversial figure, awards marks out of twenty-five for the piping and drumming combined. The reason for the third Judge is that it was felt too often that the drummers were concentrating on impressing their particular judge and overlooking the necessity of playing in conjunction with their pipers.

Champion of Champions League

There are four grades of pipe band, organised in what is known as the Champion of Champions League. Grade one consists of twenty bands; there are around sixty bands in grade two; and in grades three and four the numbers are well into three figures and still increasing. This is a remarkably popular pastime, not only in Scotland but throughout the world, and piping is steadily increasing in popularity on a world scale.

Individual Pipers

The individual pipers regard themselves, and with

good reason, as the most important part of any Highland Games. There are usually three sections under which they can compete. The foremost of these is the Piobreachdh, or Pibroch. In addition to the Pibroch which is the most highly regarded form of pipe playing, the individual pipers may also compete in playing a march or a strathspey.

Playing the Piobreachdh, or Pibroch

This is the truly classical music of the pipes, composed generally to mark some historic event, as for instance the birth of a son to the clan chieftain. The winning of the Pibroch playing is considered the greatest achievement in any Games and the prizes are commensurate. While playing the Pibroch the piper marches slowly in sympathy with his music, although not necessarily in time with it. The Pibroch may last from around five to as long as twenty minutes, reflecting the mood of the subject. The judge listens for four particular elements: the timing, i.e. the tempo or speed of the piping; the execution, i.e. the fingering and the grace notes; the expression and the tuning, i.e the pipes must be in tune.

Playing the March

Even if less highly regarded than the Pibroch, such competitions are still a considerable test of a piper's skills. When playing a march the piper marches round in time to the stirring martial music, and to the less knowledgeable this may present a more impressive spectacle than the playing of the Pibroch.

Playing the Strathspeys

The third competition for individual pipers is the playing of strathspeys and reels, the familiar dance music played for the competitive dancing. For these tunes the piper remains standing still, tapping his foot in time to the music. Each of these various types of individual piping is generally judged by two or more judges.

Scottish Official Board of Highland Dancing

Highland dancing is another very popular feature. Since 1950 when the Scottish Official Board of Highland Dancing (SOBHD) was formed, the dancers at any sanctioned competition around the world know that the steps they are dancing are the same everywhere and that they will be recognised by the judges and the other dancers.

Judges

The judges must be members of the examining bodies of the SOBHD, namely the Scottish Dance Teachers Alliance, the British Association of Teachers of Dancing, and the UK Alliance of Teachers, as well as affiliated groups around the world. They must pass a comprehensive written examination and judging tests in order to become eligible to join the panels of judges from which judges are selected for each event. No teachers of dancing may judge their own students, and no competitors their own age group. The SOBHD requires three judges each to assess and score each competitor independently of the others.

Highland Fling

Half a dozen or so different forms of dance may be seen at Highland Games. Of these the best known, perhaps, is the Highland Fling, reputed to have originated as a shepherd lad's imitation of a courting stag on the hill. The Highland Fling is danced by one person standing on the spot, with

53

arms raised above the head to simulate the stag's antlers.

Sword Dance
Almost as well known is the *Gille Calum*, as it is termed in Gaelic, better known as the Sword Dance. Reputedly originated by Malcolm Canmore, who crossed his sword over another captured from a defeated enemy then danced over them (*see* p.15), the Sword Dance is still danced over the crossed blades of two swords. If the dancer touches the swords during the dance points are forfeited and if either is displaced the dancer is disqualified.

Hullachan, or Reel of Tulloch
The *Hullachan*, a reel danced by four men, supposedly originated in the Inverness-shire village of Tulloch, when the Minister was late for the service one Sabbath and the congregation started dancing to keep warm. Although dancing in fours, the dancers are judged individually on their performance in the formalised dance.

Shean Triubhs
The *Shean Triubhs*, or Old Trousers, is another Highland dance which is performed regularly at the Games. Performed by dancers in trews, its vigorous leg movements are popularly thought to symbolise the Highlanders' historic hatred of the Lowland dress (*see* p20).

Hornpipe and Irish Jig
Two other dances may often be seen at the Highland Games. The Sailor's Hornpipe is danced in a form of naval uniform and simulates the hauling on ropes, manning of the yardarm, splicing

of the mainbrace and other feats performed by seamen under sail. The Irish Jig is performed in a stylised red and green outfit. Danced to the tune of 'Paddy's Leather Breeches' and 'The Irish Washerwoman' it symbolises Paddy's rage at his breeches being shrunk by a washerwoman and her spirited defiance at the attack on her competence as a washerwoman.

Aboyne Dress
Since the kilt is essentially a male garment and the sight of women dancers wearing the kilt was felt to be improper, some of the old Highland Games Societies, notably those at Lonach, Braemar, Glenisla, and Aboyne, decided to introduce a new dress for female competitors. In 1953 this new form of dress, based on a seventeenth-century female costume, was introduced at the Aboyne Games. The Aboyne dress is longer than the kilt, although short enough to allow the judges to see the leg movements and judge them accordingly. The dance Flora Macdonald's Fancy was revived to be danced by ladies wearing the Aboyne dress. To see children from seven to thirteen or fourteen years of age dressed in a travesty of the male Highland garb and liberally bedecked with badges won as prizes in various competitions, even when dancing faultlessly, cannot compare with the sight of an attractive lass in a suitable dress also performing well.

Judging the Dancing
The above dances are judged out of eighty points for technique, with deportment and timing gaining ten points each. Five points are lost for touching a sword in the Sword Dance, and the competitor is disqualified if a sword is displaced. Competitors

in the dancing are also disqualified if any part of their dress, or accoutrements, should fall off during their performance.

Games Field
If there is a sufficiently large area available, the Games field is divided into some four or more equal portions. This allows some or all of the foregoing events to take place at the same time, so that there is always something of interest happening for everyone present. In the larger Games it can sometimes be rather like a six-ring circus, with everything happening at once and hardly time to take it all in. In such cases, however, the spectators can usually find a position where they can watch whichever events they wish in turn, or else obtain a central viewing point from which they can switch their gaze from one event to another at will.

Events Outside the Ring
Certain Highland Games include other events, which take place outside the ring. One of the most common is a marathon, or hill climbing race, which is always popular where there is a convenient hill nearby. Some Highland Games also include cycle racing on grass which is quite different from road racing and presents some interesting problems. These may or may not be outside the ring and the same applies where trotting horse events are included. Those Games which include gymkhana events may also set a separate area aside for them. It is perhaps in the smaller Games that the most interesting variations will be found, rifle or clay pigeon shooting, even horse racing on a small scale. The Newburgh Games in Fife even includes coble racing on the River Tay, attracting a considerable entry. All of these by their very

nature must be conducted outside the main ring, although none the less an important feature of the Games themselves.

Novelty Events
Most Games include some novelty events, such as an obstacle race, with slippery poles, nets pegged to the ground, hanging tyres, or revolving drums and so on, to be negotiated by the competitors. Alternatively there may be a sack race, or a pillow fight with straw-filled sacks using one hand only while sitting astride a caber raised from the ground, providing good sport for the spectators and contestants alike. Stilt races and kilted races, or tilting the bucket from a wheelbarrow armed with a pole, with the penalty of being soaked for failure are also popular at some Games, while at Lonach there is a prize for the best-dressed Highlander. Before the 1914 war a game of Shinty was sometimes played as well. The essence of the Highland Games has always been variety.

Other Attractions
In addition to the usual refreshment marquees, there are often other side-shows of interest. Highland craftsmen display and demonstrate their crafts: horn-handled crook making, kilt making, shoeing, and ornamental smith-work; picture galleries exhibiting Highland scenes; even the latest examples of four-wheeled-drive vehicles – all these and more may be seen at the Games. It is the infinite variety to be found at the Games, from north to south, east to west, which has such a wide appeal.

Overseas Tent
Highland Games have now become so popular

internationally that some Games have an Overseas Tent. Visitors from overseas, whether of Scottish extraction or not, are welcomed by the organisers, or officials delegated for the purpose, who will do their best to help them to have an enjoyable day. Clan Society officers of various Clan Societies are sometimes present too, willing and ready to greet their fellow clan members. The spread of the Highland Games around the world has thus helped to foster a worldwide interest in the Scottish heritage.

Highland Games Outside Scotland

Nowadays it is almost essential for successful contestants to take part in the Highland Games on either side of the Atlantic. Nor is it uncommon for contestants from 'down under' to enter the Games successfully in Scotland, or indeed in North America. Scandinavians, Dutch, Swedes, South Africans, Belgians, Australians, New Zealanders, Canadians, Americans, Japanese and Fijians all have competed with varying degrees of success in Scottish Highland Games. Games have been held and are held regularly as far afield as Hong Kong and Jakarta, in Australia, New Zealand, South Africa, Canada and the USA. North Carolina's Grandfather Mountain Highland Games, established in 1956 and growing from strength to strength each year, has become a notable international occasion and an example of the modern trend. The world-wide explosion of interest in the Highland Games in the last two decades has been a remarkable phenomenon.

Local Variations Overseas

In the same way that the Games in Scotland tend to have a local flavour, so the Games overseas also have a tendency to include some local touches. One interesting test to be found in Canada and the USA is the 'Farmer's Walk' in which a competitor has to lift two stones, weighing 200 pounds or more each, and walk as far as he can. Kilted golf matches before or after the Games are a feature of some North American Games. Such unusual competitions as Scottish deerhound coursing, cairn terrier racing, Scottish dogs contests, may be included in some parts of North America. Haggis hurling and a 'bonniest knees' competition with a blindfold female judge are features of yet other Games in the USA. Log cutting, sheep shearing, tomahawk throwing, pigeon racing, seven-a-side rugby, five-a-side football and Scottish baking are all unusual features of Games in different parts of the world providing a definite local interest. This is what the Games were originally intended to provide and this is probably one of the explanations for the remarkable international increase in interest in them over the past two decades.

A Highland Spectacle
Like their counterparts in Scotland, they provide anyone with Scots blood – and indeed many who have not a drop of Scottish blood in their veins – with a good reason for having a day out and enjoying themselves amongst local friends while savouring a uniquely Scottish and Highland spectacle.

Camanachd, or Shinty

Historians

The Reverend Father J. Ninian MacDonald, OSB, of St Benedict's Abbey, Fort Augustus, rightly deserves the title of first historian of *camanachd*, the game of shinty. He both played and studied the game throughout most of his life. His book *Shinty: A Short History of the Ancient Highland Game* was published in 1932. According to him the history of Shinty could be traced back to as far as around 2000 BC. In his view one of the outstanding features of the game was that it had resisted anything savouring of professionalism and had always been devoid of any form of class distinction: from the chieftain to the lowest clansmen, all had vied in equal terms. 'On the turf, as under the turf, all men are equal.' Roger Hutchinson's definitive book *Camanachd: The Story of Shinty*, published in 1989, brings the history up to date with all the detail anyone interested in the game could wish.

The Cuchullin Saga

The Cuchullin Saga, which dates from around AD 1, tells of the young Cuchullin, an early Scottish hero, outstanding as a shinty player. In order to complete his training in arms, Cuchullin 'was sent by his uncle to be instructed in a celebrated school in the island of Skye, which was conducted by a female warrior, the Lady Scathach – On his arrival at Scathach's mansion he found a number of her pupils and other warriors engaged in a game of *camanachd* outside the gates of the fortress. He joined issue with them and defeated them.'

Lord Lovat's Comments
After reading Father Ninian MacDonald's book, the late Lord Lovat wrote:

> Older players who look back to the New Year and 'Old' New Year games of shinty as played between neighbouring parishes will find the description of Cuchullin's games . . . reminiscent in shape and form to the battles (they could rightly bear no other name) which were fought to the tune of the pipes, to the stimulant of *uisge beatha*, and for the admiration of, and for that matter with the active assistance of, the lady spectators. No regulation as to numbers; no differentiation between the stroke made with the hand, foot, or caman; a goal equally vulnerable from the rear as from the front; no minor matters such as boundaries, time-keeping, or off-side; the arrival of fresh contingents and the departure of the unsatisfied; all are common to the game of forty years ago as they were to the classic encounters of the past . . .

Games with Stick and Ball
In his book Father Ninian claimed that the use of a bat, club, or similar instrument with a ball was a feature peculiar to the Celtic nations. He concluded that

> hockey, golf, cricket, stool-ball, trap-ball, tip-cat, *et hoc genus omne*, no matter by what names they are now differentiated, no matter what modifications they may have suffered in the lapse of centuries, no matter what special

rules of play may have crystallised around this or that individual variety and caused it eventually to stand out distinct from the others – all reveal an unmistakable community of origin – New names have been given to many of these varieties simply by ringing the changes on the caman, the club used in the original game – The Gaelic *caman* is merely a bent stick, or club, hockey is the hooked-stick, La Crosse is the crook, etc. Likewise the most favoured derivation of cricket is from 'crice' an old English word for crook, and early illustrations of the game manifest the curved nature of the bat then employed.

Camack

Father Ninian also pointed out that the term 'shinty' had only come into being in recent years in general use amongst English speakers, whereas before the Gaelic speakers had always referred to *camack*. As proof he quoted an extract from the Edinburgh *Evening Courant* for 22 January 1821: 'On Christmas and New Year's Day matches were played at camack . . .' The word 'shinty' itself he claimed was possibly derived from the old Celtic word 'shin' to play, although the *Oxford English Dictionary* refers to the cry used in the game: 'Shin ye, shin your side!' – apparently admonitions to a player attempting to approach on the wrong side.

The Ancient Game

He also claimed that the *camanachd* played in his day and two thousand years ago were essentially one and the same game:

The Ball
It was played with a ball . . . about four

inches in diameter made of some light elastic material such as woollen yarn wound round and round sand covered with leather. Sometimes a rounded piece of wood, a ball of twisted hair, or knob from the trunk of a tree, carefully fashioned into a globular shape was substituted.

The Club

Each player had a wooden club with which to strike the ball; it was frequently made of ash, about three feet in length, carefully shaped and smoothed, and with the lower ends flat and curved and it was usually called a caman, cammoc, or camman, though we also find in the old writings lorg . . . later a shinny, shinty . . . etc.

The Players and Pitch

In a regular match the players in either side were equal in number. It was played on a more or less level and grassy field or plain. At each end of the delimited ground the boundary or objective was clearly designated. Sometimes this object consisted merely of a gap in a hedge or wall, sometimes it was the space between two trees, bushes, poles, or other fixed objects. The length of territory between the objective of one party and that of the other varied considerably – from a hundred yards to several miles.

The Start

The game was begun by throwing up the ball in the middle of the field of play; this was done by some neutral person; alternatively the ball was buried in the sand. The players endeavoured to drive the ball with their camans towards their objective, each party, of course, in an opposite direction.

The Finish

Whichever party succeeded in first reaching a boundary, or goal, was adjudged to have scored a *leth-bhaire* (lit. half a goal). The teams then made a volte face or about turn and exchanged objectives. If the previous scorers succeeded in driving the ball again to the objective they were deemed to have scored a *bhaire* (full goal) and the contest came to an end.

The Back, or Rear-Guard

It was customary for each party to station one of its most skilful players in close proximity to the boundary which it was endeavouring to defend. It was this player's duty to intercept that ball should it happen to come flying in his direction and he was said to stand *cul*, or *cul-bhaire*. (Back or rear-guard.)

1666

Although there is no reason to doubt the accuracy of Father Ninian's observations, unfortunately he does not give many dates or references to substantiate his conclusions. He does, however, note the mention of shinty playing in the 1666 Kirk Session records of Kinnedar in Morayshire, which appears to be the first reference that can be accurately checked.

1769

The next reference to be found is probably that in Thomas Pennant's *Tour of Scotland* in 1769: 'Of the ancient sports of the Highlands, those retained are throwing the stone of strength (*clach neart*) which occasions emulation, who can throw it the furthest; the shinty, or striking a ball of wood, or hair;

64

this game is played between two parties furnished with clubs in a large plain; whichever side strikes it first to their own goal wins the match.'

1793
In the Statistical Account for the Parish of Moulin in Perthshire in 1793 there was the following:

It is observable that those gymnastic exercises which constituted the chief pastime of the Highlands forty or fifty years ago, have almost entirely disappeared. At every fair or meeting of the country people there were contests of racing, wrestling, putting the stone, etc and on holidays all the males of the district, young and old, met to play at . . . shinty. These games are now practised only by schoolboys having given place to the more elegant though less manly amusement of dancing. Note: shinty is game played with sticks crooked at the end and a ball of wood.

1810
It is also interesting to note various references to shinty in the Press of the nineteenth century. For instance, in 1810 in the Annual Register there is a rather condescending note, more understandable when one bears in mind that Scotland was then referred to simply as North Britain: 'Contending parties in the northern counties of England exert themselves to drive the Shinny to its goal.'

1821
More to the point was the report in the Edinburgh *Evening Courier* of 22 January 1821:

On Tuesday last, one of the most spirited

camack matches witnessed for many years in this country (Badenoch) where that manly sport of our forefathers has been regularly kept up during the Christmas festivities, took place in the extensive meadows below the inn at Pitmain ... On Christmas and New Year's Day matches were played in the policy below the house of Drakies at the camack ... which were conducted with great spirit.

Dornoch

In his book *Memorabilia Domestica* the Reverend Donald Sage described shinty being played in Dornoch around the beginning of the nineteenth century:

The Shinty, or Shinny, a ball of wood, was inserted into the ground, and the leaders with their clubs struck at it, until they got it out again. The heat of the game then began. The one party laboured hard and most keenly to drive the ball to the opposite point, or baile, and the other to drive it across the boundary to the starting point; and which party soever did either, carried the day. In my younger days the game was universal in the north. Men of all ages amongst the working classes joined in it, especially on Old New Year's Day. I distinctly remember seeing on such joyous occasions at Dornoch the whole male populations, from the grey-haired grandfather to the lightest heeled stripling, turn out to the links, each with his club; and from eleven o'clock in the forenoon till it became dark, they would keep at it with all the keenness accompanied by shouts, with which their forefathers had wielded the claymore ...

1841

In Barron's *Northern Highlands in the 19th Century*
the following is recorded for 23 June 1841:

> Highlanders in London were greatly inter-
> ested in a shinty match organised by the
> committee of a body which called itself 'The
> Society of True Highlanders'. The match took
> place in the Copenhagen Fields, an extent
> of rich meadowland lying on the outskirts
> of Islington. There was much enthusiasm
> and keenly contested games. It is said that
> before the gathering half the glens in Lochaber
> had been ransacked for shinty clubs. In the
> evening there was a dinner at which Mr
> Forbes McNeil presided and many Northern
> gentlemen were present . . .

McIan's Clans of the Scottish Highlands

In R.R. McIan's well-known series depicting the
clans of the Scottish Highlands, first published in
1845, Grant of Glenmoriston is shown holding a
ball and a caman with the following description:

> He is in the attitude of throwing the ball at the
> commencement if the game of Camanachd,
> or Shinnie, as it is named in the low country.
> This exhilarating amusement is very popular
> amongst the Highlanders; two opposing par-
> ties endeavour by means of the camac, or
> club, to drive the ball to a certain spot on the
> other side, and the distance is sometimes so
> great that a whole day's exertion is required
> to play out the game. A vigorous runner, it
> is obvious, has a great advantage; but agility
> is not the only requisite; a great skill in
> preventing the ball being driven to the desired

goal is necessary, and many awkward blows and falls take place during the contest. Differing parishes frequently turn out to try their abilities at this exciting game and no better exercise could be enjoyed on a winter's day. When there is a numerous meeting the field has much the appearance of a battle scene; there are banners flying, bagpipes playing and a keen melee around the ball. Young and old, rich and poor, join in this athletic sport, and though it is usually engaged *con amor*, prizes are frequently contended for.

Shinty in Canada

The many Highlanders who emigrated to Canada from the late eighteenth century onwards took their Highland games with them, including, of course, shinty, or *camanachd*. Although the game was originally played in the old Highland fashion, like many other traditions it was gradually adapted to the new circumstances in which the settlers found themselves. The large stretches of flat ice which formed on the rivers and lakes in the winter provided an ideal surface for the game. Crude early skates, formed from steel runners screwed to a wooden board and strapped to the feet, were used by the players. From this there developed the national sport of ice hockey, which began in the 1840s in this way at Kingston, Ontario. *Camanachd*, or shinty, itself continued in some areas, but the origins, the rules, and even the name were largely forgotten. It is only in recent years that there has been something of a revival, in Nova Scotia at least.

Mid-Nineteenth Century Decline

Despite the enthusiasm of keen supporters of the

game it began to fall into decline during the mid-nineteenth century and there was apparently a real danger that it might have been allowed to lapse altogether. Part of the trouble seemed to stem from the variations in the rules, which differed greatly from glen to glen. For instance, the length of the caman itself was anything but uniform. Although a long club used in both hands was most common, the players in Kintyre, for instance, favoured a short club held in one hand only. In some places it was forbidden to carry the ball or throw it by hand. 'Crapachs' were, however, permissible by which the player might catch the ball in mid-air, throw it up and hit it with his caman. Another name for this stroke was 'fornaird'.

Chisholm of Glassburn's Rules and Regulations

In 1880 Captain Chisholm of Glassburn drew up *The Constitution, Rules and Regulations of the Strathglass Shinty Club* and it is to him that the very survival of the game is due. Contrary to the modern rules these allowed: 'The ball, if caught in the air, may be thrown or run with even through the hails (and the person running must be caught and not tripped by club or feet, but whenever caught must throw the ball, or drop it) or it may be thrown from one to another as long as it does not touch the ground.' The method of scoring was twenty-five points for a hail, or goal, and if the ball was driven over the goal line, or over the bar, it counted one point. Some idea of the fierceness of the games then played may, however, be gained by reading between the lines of the rule quoted above.

The Kilt v Knickerbockers

Throughout the 1880s, although the popularity of shinty was definitely increasing, there were numerous disputes amongst the various clubs and teams, not the least of which concerned the proper garb for the game. Some resolutely held that the kilt should be worn and others held that knickerbockers were more decent in the case of a player being knocked down. While tempers and discussion waxed hot on such matters the game continued to gain supporters. It was clearly reaching the stage where it had to become properly organised.

Formation of the Camanachd Association

In 1888 the Strathglass Code of Rules was re-published with emendations. At that time they played twenty-one a side, with a field of 300 by 200 yards to allow plenty of room. During the late 1870s the hair ball finally gave way to one covered in leather such as is used today. By 1892 there were around forty flourishing clubs in existence in the Highlands and as far south as London, including not only the London Scottish, but also the London and Northern Counties. In 1893 a general meeting of all supporters of the game was convened at Kingussie and the Camanachd Association was formed; Captain Chisholm of Glassburn was nominated the first chieftain of the Association and Simon, Lord Lovat, first President.

Influence of the Highland Regiments

There is little doubt that the Highland regiments played their own part in perpetuating shinty as a game. As they regularly introduced Highland Games at their various postings, so they also played shinty wherever they could find wood suitable for making shinty sticks. During the Boer War, indeed, twenty-four camans were standard issue for the Highland regiments. Having played the game keenly when in the army, it was likely that demobilised soldiers would continue to play the game on their return to civilian life, and this must have encouraged an interest in the game.

University Shinty
An Aberdeen University Shinty Club was founded as early as 1861. It appears initially to have been very much an internal affair restricted to playing on the links of Old Aberdeen and not venturing further afield. Their first fixture outside Aberdeen seems to have been in 1889. This appears to have inspired Edinburgh University to form a Shinty Club in 1891, which was resoundingly defeated by Aberdeen in 1892. Inter-university games then continued and in 1901 Glasgow University also formed their own Shinty Club. Finally all were affiliated to the Camanachd Association.

The 1920s and 1930s
During the 1920s and 1930s there was an attempt to introduce competition between Irish hurling teams and Scottish shinty teams. There was even talk of evolving a set of compromise rules for the two games, for the standardisation of the stick (the hurling stick being broader) and of the ball, which is larger in hurling. These came to nothing, which was unfortunate for shinty, which never drew the large crowds of spectators that followed Irish hurling. However in 1937 the Schools Camanachd Association was formed and junior shinty continued to spread the game's popularity.

Modern Shinty
In modern shinty the teams consist of twelve players a side, playing on a field from 140 yards to 170 yards long and 70 to 80 yards wide, but

preferably not less than 160 by 80 yards. The goal posts are twelve feet apart and ten feet high with a cross-bar and nets attached. A ten–yard area is marked out in front of each goal, also a penalty spot twenty yards in front of each goal. The head of the caman must be able to pass through a ring two and a half inches in diameter. The ball is cork, covered with leather, no larger than eight inches in circumference and weighing three ounces. Players may not wear spikes or tackets. Each game lasts ninety minutes with forty-five minutes each way and a five–minute break in the middle.

State of the Game Today
Although now strictly controlled by rules, shinty remains a spirited game, fast, and requiring both staying power and excellent ball control. With pipers at the sidelines and a fiercely partisan audience, it still has all the essentials noted in the Cuchullin Saga. It is still essentially the original Highland game from which it would appear many other ball games have sprung. It has retained its popularity in much of the Highlands, even if sadly there are areas where it is no longer played as it once was and, even worse, some where it has lapsed completely. It has now reached the stage, however, where a regular League Championship is played annually among a number of keenly competing teams from various areas throughout the Highlands, with sponsorship from major names such as Glenmorangie, the Bank of Scotland and Unilever. The future for the game seems assured, with younger players coming on and, at last, a mutually advantageous union with the Irish game of hurling looking ever more likely.

The 56lb weight-over-the-bar event has been compared to tossing a
7 year-old child over a double-decker bus.

Throwing the hammer on a windy day, and
below a team in the throes of a gruelling tug-of-war.

Tossing the caber , which weighs an average of 150lbs,
takes a gritty competitor.

The Games in North America: *above* Stone-carrying (580lbs' worth) and sheaf-tossing at the New Hampshire Games.

Caber-tossing at Fergus Scottish Festival, and *right* the Antigonish Kilted Golf Tournament, both in Canada.

left In Orlando, Florida, the children's games have a Goofy overseer.

below It is wise to get a hat and keep your cool in the sticky heat of the Jakarta Highland Gathering in Indonesia.

Also at Jakarta, the tug-of-war draws a considerable crowd.

above Students at the Coady International Institute bring an exotic air to the annual Antigonish Games parade.

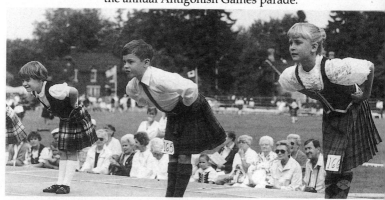

At Fergus, participants of all ages compete as dancers, and of course no Games is complete without a pipe band.

above Shinty is one of the world's oldest and most dynamic team sports. Cycling is a tamer but equally hotly contested event.

Queen Elizabeth II, a traditional visitor to the Braemar Gathering, present
a champion with his trophy.

The Highland Games in Scotland

There are around sixty-two Highland Games in Scotland run under the aegis of the Scottish Games Association offering cash prizes to competitors. Some events may be restricted to local entrants or open to all-comers. Roughly half as many Amateur Games are run under Olympic Rules supervised by the Scottish Amateur Athletic Association. Whether Professional or Amateur, competitor or spectator, those who make the circuit of the Highland Games throughout Scotland enjoy some of the finest scenery to be had, not only during their travels, but also at the sites of the various Games themselves, for they are usually extremely well situated. Taking them alphabetically here are some details of the locations of the more important and interesting Games.

Details of Games and Organisers
Since the organisers tend to change annually no addresses have been given. The Scottish Tourist Board provides advance details of most of the Highland Games held in Scotland each year, in their *Events in Scotland* booklet, which includes the names and addresses of the current organisers, but sometimes individual Games may not have advised the Tourist Board sufficiently far in advance to be included.
Further particulars may be obtained from:
Mr Andrew Rettie, The Secretary, The Scottish

Games Association, 24 Florence Place, Perth PH1
5BW *Tel*: 0738 2778. The SGA also publish an
annual Year Book including details of all the
Professional Highland Games held in Scotland,
obtainable from Mr Rettie. Particulars of the
Amateur Highland Games are obtainable from: The
Scottish Amateur Athletic Association, Caledonia
House, South Gyle, Edinburgh EH1 9DQ *Tel*: 031-
317 7320/7321.

Aberdeen

Aberdeen has the northernmost university in
Britain and is the third largest city in Scotland.
The Highland Games are organised by the City
Corporation and are generally held in June in the
Hazelhead Park in the west end of the 'granite
city', now the bustling oil capital of Scotland.
The chieftain of the Games, appropriately, is
Lady Aberdeen. A major attraction is the World
Caber Tossing Championship, attracting contest-
ants from all parts of the world.

Aberfeldy

This is a very pleasant small and sleepy town on
the banks of the Tay, thirty-two miles west of Perth.
Usually held in mid-August, the Games, officially
entitled 'The Atholl and Breadalbane Highland
Gathering', were first held in 1843, and are now
pleasantly combined with the local agricultural
show. The show and stock judging takes place
in the morning and the Games in the afternoon.
Although this Gathering lapsed in the 1930s, it
was duly revived in the 1970s and is now held
in the town's Victoria Park in a very picturesque
setting looking across the River Tay to the serried
mountain peaks in the distance.

Aberlour

In the famous Speyside whisky-distilling area seventeen miles south-west of Keith, these Games, currently held early in August, are officially called 'The Aberlour and Strathspey Highland Games'. They are held in the Alice Littler Park above the Spey itself between the Conval Hills and Ben Rinnes (2,755 ft), within easy range of several well-known distilleries. Unusual in that these Games were started during the 1939–45 war by the local Home Guard, they have Sir Ewan Macpherson-Grant as chieftain and are notable in including a sheep dog trial.

Abernethy

The Abernethy Highland Games and Clan Grant Rally are usually held on the Saturday before 12 August amidst beautiful surroundings on the playing field at Nethy Bridge, a small village five miles south-west of Grantown-on-Spey. In addition to these Amateur Games, there is always a chance of seeing an osprey passing overhead from the well-known nesting site at nearby Boat of Garten. The Games generally continue from 10.30 to 17.00.

Aboyne

On Deeside, eleven miles east of Ballater, these Games were started in 1867 under the auspices of the famous all-round athlete and heavyweight champion Donald Dinnie and are usually held on the first Saturday in August. The Dinnie Trophy is awarded to the winner of the heavyweight events. The Marquis of Huntly is chieftain of the Games. Held on the village green, they are rightly regarded today as one of the more famous Games. From 9.30 onwards piping; 12.30–17.30 Official Games.

Airdrie
A Lanarkshire industrial centre eleven miles east of Glasgow, these Amateur Games are generally held in early June.

Airth
This small Central Lowland village lies eight miles south of Stirling in the old coal-mining area on the south side of the River Forth. The Games first started in the 1870s and are always held on the fourth Saturday in July. An unusual feature is the pony trotting.

Alva
This small town is in Clackmannanshire, seven miles east of Stirling and nestling immediately under the Ochil Hills. The Games are usually held in early July and include a hill race to the top of Dumyat Hill (1,375 ft) and back, which attracts keen hill racers from considerable distances.

Arbroath
Arbroath is a large burgh and seaport seventeen miles north-east of Dundee. These Games, held in the town's Victoria Park, generally in mid-July, feature the usual heavy events, piping and dancing as well as cycling. They start at 13.00 and continue until 17.00.

Ardrossan
This Ayrshire seaport and holiday centre thirty-one miles south-west of Glasgow has a ferry service to the Isle of Arran. The Games are usually held in mid-June in the Laighdykes Playing Fields from 12.00 to 17.30.

Argyllshire Gathering
See Oban

Arisaig
This small, sheltered crofting township geared to
the tourist industry is seven miles south of Mallaig
on the west coast. The Games are generally held
in late July close to the sea and the famous Sil-
ver Sands of Arisaig, an outstandingly beautiful
location. This is a very sporting small Highland
occasion where the Gaelic will still be heard
amongst the competitors and spectators. Usually
held from midday onwards.

Assynt Gathering
See Lochinver

Ballater
Seventeen miles east of Braemar on Deeside, these
Games were started in 1864 when the village was
gaining popularity as a Victorian spa. Its other
claim to fame was as the station nearest to
Balmoral. The Games are usually held in mid-
August in Monaltrie Park surrounded by purple
heather-clad hills. The hill race up nearby Craig
Colleach (600 ft) is a particular feature of the
day. The chieftain is Farquharson of Invercauld.
These are the first of the notable Deeside Highland
Games. Generally held from 12.30 to 17.30.

Balloch
This is a small village favourably situated at the
foot of Loch Lomond with a railway station and
a pierhead on the loch. It lies four miles north
of Dumbarton at the south end of Loch Lomond,

just to the north of the Highland Line. The Games are generally held in pleasant parkland in Christie Park, Alexandria, in mid-July, and include a pipe band competition and special heavyweight competition. Coincidental with the Glasgow Trades holidays and being only twenty miles from Glasgow this is liable to be a very popular event. Dancing and piping start at 11.00.

Balquhidder, Lochearnhead and Strathyre Highland Games
See Lochearnhead

Bathgate
A bustling market town in West Lothian, almost midway between Edinburgh and Glasgow, these Amateur Games feature a hill race and are generally held towards the end of May.

Bearsden and Milngavie
In Dunbartonshire north-west of Glasgow, these Amateur Games are usually held in early June.

Birnam
Birnam is tiny in comparison with the nearby well-known and flourishing village of Dunkeld, which is geared to tourism, although now bypassed by the main road from Perth to Inverness. Birnam lives very much in the shadow of its larger neighbour, but these Games were started there as early as 1865. They are usually held in late August just half a mile south of Dunkeld across the River Tay in pleasant parkland beside the river itself.

Blackford
About nine miles north-east of Dunblane in the

Perthshire hills, these Games are held in the Blackford Games Park not far from the Tullibardine malt whisky distillery. A particular feature of note is the Scottish Tug-of-War Championships. Generally held in late May from 13.00 to 17.00.

Blairgowrie

In the centre of the soft fruit growing area of Perthshire these Games are of comparatively recent origin. They are, however, well placed and attract a considerable crowd of spectators. They are generally held on the first Sunday in September after the Braemar Games.

Braemar

The world-famous Braemar Gathering originated around 1800; royal patronage dates from Queen Victoria's first visit in 1848 and is now a recognised feature of the day. Lying in a natural bowl in the hills, eight miles from Balmoral, the Gathering attracts spectators and competitors from all round the world as well as Scots from a wide area. It is a considerable international occasion. Organised by the Braemar Highland Society, it is usually held on the first Saturday in September and is the last of the big Games and a worthy climax to the season. It starts at 10.00 and ends at 17.00. Bookings open on 1 February.

Bridge of Allan

On the Allan Water a couple of miles or so north-west of Stirling and nestling beneath the Ochil Hills, these Amateur Games naturally include a hill race. They are generally held in early August and attract a good entry.

Brodick

A popular holiday village on the east coast of the

Isle of Arran with a pier facing the mainland. The Amateur Games are currently held early in August in the Ormidale Park from 13.30 to 17.00.

Burntisland
This royal burgh and seaport, once regarded by James IV along with other ports in the Forth as one of the 'Jewels in his Crown', is now a holiday centre on the north shore of the Firth of Forth between Aberdour and Kinghorn in Fife. The Games are generally held in late July, from 12.00 to 17.00, in a park beneath Binn Hill (632 ft). Supposedly dating from the year 1635, they are now regarded as a traditional Fife holiday. The Binn race is only open to locals. The Games coincide with the Edinburgh Trades holidays and are thus generally extremely well attended.

Bute
See Rothesay

Caithness
See Thurso and Halkirk

Campbeltown
See Southend

Carmunnock
See Glasgow

Carrick
See Girvan

Ceres
This small north Fife village is a little more than two

miles south of Cupar. It is claimed these Games originated after Bannockburn in 1314 which would make them amongst the oldest in Scotland even if not strictly Highland. They are held in late June in a natural amphitheatre in the centre of the village, known as Bow Butts Park, with a burn running through it. Features include horse racing on a minor scale and cycle racing.

Cortachy
This is a small village some five miles north of Kirriemuir in Angus and adjacent to the Earl of Airlie's estates. The Games are held in early August in a magnificent natural setting beside the River Prosen, with a fine view of Airlie Castle. Very much a local affair with a friendly atmosphere and features such as a flower show.

Cowal
See Dunoon

Crieff
In the Perthshire hills well placed above the River Earn, this town is a well-known tourist and health resort. Dating back to 1870, the Games have a very varied programme including cycling as well as the usual events. An important feature is the Scottish Heavyweight Championships, which brings together the top international competitors. The Games are usually well attended being equally easily accessible from Edinburgh and Glasgow. They are generally held in mid-August from 12.00 to 17.00.

Cupar
A good solid Scots county town, about which

there is a somewhat double-edged saying: 'He who maun to Cupar, maun to Cupar,' indicating that 'All roads lead to Cupar.' The Cupar Amateur Highland Games are usually held in early July from 13.00 to 17.30 in the Duffus Park, and include heavies, field, track, piping and dancing events, amusement and refreshment stalls.

Dingwall
The capital of Ross and Cromarty, Dingwall is an attractive small Highland town at the foot of the Cromarty Firth, straddling the routes to the north and west. The Games are usually held in mid-July in the Jubilee Park from 11.00 to 17.00. *Contact*: Ross and Cromarty Tourist Board, North Kessock (*Tel*: 0463 73505) for further details.

Dornoch
The capital of Sutherland and still basically an attractive sleepy old medieval cathedral town on the north shore of the Dornoch Firth, this royal burgh is also a popular holiday resort. The Games are usually held before 12 August in the Meadows Park from 10.30 to 17.00.

Drumtochty
Laurencekirk is a small market town twenty-five miles south of Aberdeen in Kincardineshire. The Games are generally held in late June the grounds of Drumtochty Castle from 12.00 to 17.30.

Dufftown Highland Games
Dufftown is known as 'the whisky capital of Scotland' with seven distilleries ringing the town. The Games are currently held in late July from 11.00 to 17.00 in the Mortlach School Field within sight and scent of at least two distilleries.

Dunbeath

This is a small coastal village and harbour in Caithness midway between Lybster and Helmsdale, eighteen miles south-west of Wick. It was one of the coastal villages established by the Duke of Sutherland during the notorious Clearances, when the inhabitants of the townships of Kildonan and Strathnaver were evicted and herded into villages by the sea. The Games started in 1850 and still maintain a high standard despite the smallness of the community. They are traditionally held on the third Friday in July and are followed by a dance in the evening.

Dundee

The fourth-largest city in Scotland, Dundee is well placed at the mouth of the River Tay. Currently held early in July in the Caird Park Stadium, these Games were established as recently as 1970. Aiming principally at tourists, the organisers include professional cycling on banked tracks, in addition to such features as pipe band competitions and the British Tug-of-War Championships.

Dunoon

The principal holiday resort on the Cowal peninsula with a regular ferry service from Gourock, Dunoon is a favourite place for Glaswegians especially. The well-known Cowal Highland Gathering is held here, usually over the weekend in late August in the Stadium, and is well attended since these Amateur Games include one of the five Pipe Band Championships, which qualifies the winners for the Champion of Champions League.

Durness

This small village lies in the north-west corner

of Sutherland close to Cape Wrath. The Games were revived in the late 1960s and are generally held towards the end of July from 12.00 to 17.00 on the Shore Park with impressive views of craggy cliffs towering above. A visit to these Games could be regarded as worth it alone for the simply stupendous views of the Sutherland mountains and straths when approaching and departing.

Echt

This small village near Skene, twelve miles west of Aberdeen, holds a typical combination of Agricultural Society Show and Games usually in mid-July. The Echt and District Agricultural Society Show occupies the ground in the morning, from 09.00 onwards. The Games and a gymkhana with show-jumping follow in the afternoon. With Aberdonian thriftiness they thus provide something for everyone at the minimum expense for the maximum enjoyment.

Elgin

A royal burgh and the capital of Moray, Elgin was once a cathedral town and the ruins still remain. It is now a bustling agricultural centre also geared to tourism. These Amateur Highland Games are generally held from 13.00 to 17.00 in mid-July in Morriston Park on a promontory thrusting into the River Lossie some six miles from its mouth. They feature the North of Scotland Amateur Caber Tossing Championships.

Falkirk

Almost equidistant from Edinburgh to the south-east and Glasgow to the south-west, Falkirk is still a thriving centre despite the loss of its famous ironworks. These Amateur Games are generally held in mid-July in the Callendar Park.

Fettercairn
This small agricultural erstwhile estate village nine miles north of Brechin in south-west Kincardine-shire is perhaps most notable for its triumphal arch built in 1861 and inscribed 'Victoria and Albert', and for its nearby malt whisky distillery. This is another example of a combined agricultural show and Games, usually held towards the end of July.

Forfar
This is the county town of Angus and an attractive small agricultural market town. The Games are customarily held in mid-June in the Lochside Park from 12.30 to 17.00.

Forres
A market town and royal burgh on the River Findhorn twelve miles west of Elgin in Morayshire and close to the site of Macbeth's 'blasted heath'. The Games are generally held early in July from 13.30 to 17.00 in Grant Park, an excellent natural setting. Features are the North of Scotland Amateur 3,000 Metres Championship, also the Amateur Hammer and 28 lb Championships. Various cycling events are also included.

Fort William
At the north-east end of Loch Linnhe and three miles west of Ben Nevis, the highest mountain in Scotland, Fort William is well known to tourists. A.A. Cameron, heavyweight champion from 1903

to 1914, was born here in 1877. On his death in 1951 his medals and trophies went to the West Highland Museum in the town. The Caol and Lochaber Gathering is usually held towards the end of July in the playing field beneath Ben Nevis, a fine natural setting for these Amateur Games.

Galashiels

Galashiels is a thriving mill town and municipal burgh on the Gala Water, one mile from the Tweed in Selkirkshire. In common with most other Border towns it has an annual riding of the marches. The Braw Lads Gathering and Games commemorates a victory by local Borderers over invading English forces and combines this celebration with beating the town boundaries on horseback. Along with a large train of mounted followers the 'Braw Lad and Lass' visit Abbotsford, the home of Sir Walter Scott, ford the Tweed spectacularly, and return to commemorate the marriage of Mary Tudor and James IV. A ceremony at the War Memorial follows. So far this is merely a rather spectacular Border Common Riding. Afterwards the Games are held in Netherdale Park. Started in 1930, these sometimes include such features as heavy events and highland dancing, football and a gymkhana. This is in effect a Border celebration with Highland Games events added, but like all Border Ridings well worth attending. It is generally held towards the end of June.

Galloway
See Stranraer

Girvan
This Ayrshire seaport and popular tourist centre

is twenty-one miles south of Ayr. The Carrick Lowland Gathering is held here and includes Highland Games and a fell race. Usually held in early June and starts at 12.00 and continues until 17.30.

Glasgow
These Amateur Games are currently held at Bellahouston, a suburb in the south-west of Glasgow in early August.

Glenfinnan
These Games are usually held in mid-August at the head of Loch Shiel where the Glenfinnan Memorial stands commemorating the raising of Prince Charles Edward Stuart's Standard in 1745, when the clans rallied to his support. The Games are held alongside the Memorial and entries are restricted to locals only. Despite this they are well attended, for the beauty of the setting in itself is very hard to beat and they make a very satisfactory tourist attraction, easily reached from Fort William.

Glenisla
This small village lies on the River Isla eight miles north of Alyth in west Angus. The Glenisla Highland and Friendly Society started these Games in 1865 and they are usually held towards the end of August. A steep bank beside the river forms a natural amphitheatre. This is surrounded by deerstalking and grouse moor country, hence one of the special features is a rifle shooting competition, which starts at 8.30 a.m.; another is the Mount Blair hill race. The Earl of Airlie is a regular attender. The main Games start at 13.00 and end at 18.00.

Glenrothes

One of the more successful post-war New Towns, Glenrothes was built for a mining community which was expected to expand. When the coal ran out it had to rely on its own ingenuity and industry to develop, and has done so very well. The Highland Games are currently held towards the end of July in the Warout Stadium from 12.30 to 17.30.

Glenurquhart

Held towards the end of August in the small hamlet of Drumnadrochit, a well-known tourist area close to Loch Ness and not far from the spectacular ruins of Glenurquhart Castle, these are typical Amateur Highland Games. They feature a hill race and a road race from Inverness to Glenurquhart, as well as a handicap kilted race over 440 yards. They usually start at 11.00 and end at 17.00.

Gourock

These Amateur Games are usually held in mid-May in the Gourock Park in this well-known yachting centre and tourist resort at the mouth of the River Clyde.

Grange

This small village lies four miles east of Keith in Banffshire, in the heart of the Speyside whisky distilling area. The Games are generally held in mid-June at Bankhead Farm from 13.00 to 17.00.

Grangemouth

An industrial centre on the south side of the Forth where the River Carron enters it, these Amateur Games are generally held in early September.

Grantown-on-Spey

Twelve miles north of the well-known tourist centre at Aviemore, Grantown-on-Spey above the Cairngorms is a small, attractive, grey granite market town also geared to tourism and, as the name implies, on the famous River Spey. The Games are customarily held towards the end of June in the school playing fields from 13.15 onwards.

Halkirk

This small agricultural and slate-quarrying village in Caithness six miles south of Thurso holds the annual Caithness Games. These Games are very much older than those at Thurso, which also claim to be the Caithness Games. The Halkirk Games, held in the Recreation Park towards the end of July, include a clay-pigeon shooting competition in addition to the usual events.

Helmsdale and District Highland Games

Helmsdale is a small village at the mouth of the Helmsdale River notable for its salmon fishing. This is another of those fishing villages created by the Sutherlands to re-house dispossessed crofters during the notorious nineteenth century Clearances. It is now geared to tourism. The Games are held in the latter part of August in the Couper Park from 11.00 to 17.00.

Inveraray

This is still an attractive small town, by no means spoiled. The county town of Argyll, it stands at the west end of Loch Fyne close by Inveraray Castle, the seat of the Duke of Argyll, hereditary chieftain of the Clan Campbell. This is an area geared to tourism, but well worth visiting. Originating in

1866, these Games lapsed after the 1939–45 war, but were revived in 1956. Naturally a good deal of Campbell tartan is in evidence. A feature of the Games has been the solo piping. They are held around mid-July in the Winterton Park in the grounds of Inveraray Castle from 10.30 to 17.00.

Invercharron

Between Bonar Bridge and Ardgay in Sutherland, these are the last of the full traditional Highland Games in a good Highland setting. They are generally held on the third Saturday in September and start at 10.00, going on until 17.30.

Invergarry

On the west side of Loch Ness about halfway up the loch, Invergarry is a small village geared to tourism and sport, mainly fishing and deer-stalking. The Highland Games are usually held in mid-July between 12.30 and 18.00 on the Invergarry Shinty Field.

Invergordon

This seaport town in Ross and Cromarty on the west side of the Cromarty Firth, equidistant from Tain in the north and Dingwall in the south, was once famed as the site of a Royal Navy mutiny in the First World War; it is now best known for its distillery complex. The Games date from 1921 when they were closely linked with the old Royal Naval base. They now benefit from the industrial developments in the area. The Games are generally held towards the end of August in the castle grounds from 10.30 to 17.00.

Inverkeithing

Another Fife royal burgh, Inverkeithing is four

miles south of Dunfermline on the Firth of Forth. The Games date back to a Lammas Fair held in 1652, which included a race for a 'hat and ribbon'. They lapsed in 1965, but were started again in 1972 and are usually held in early August. The race for the 'hat and ribbon' is still run, but more modern features include a large Pipe Band Championship and a Cycle Championship.

Inverness

At the junction of the Beauly and Moray Firths, the 'Capital of the Highlands' is well placed close to the northern end of the Caledonian Canal, with good road, rail and air links to Edinburgh, 190 miles to the south. The Games, generally held in the Bucht Park in mid-July, are strictly amateur, but attract considerable numbers of knowledge-able spectators and competitors from a wide area around.

Irvine

A seaport and market town on the Ayrshire coast with local industries but also geared to tourism, Irvine usually holds these Amateur Highland Games in mid-July in the Magnum Centre.

Keith

See Grange

Kenmore

In mid-Perthshire, beautifully situated at the east end of Loch Tay, this charming erstwhile estate village was built by the Marquis of Breadalbane in the eighteenth century. It could scarcely be a more delightful place to hold such a sporting event. These small evening Games, starting at 18.00

and usually held early in July, provide an amusing and enjoyable entertainment for all concerned, as should be the case in such events.

Kilmore and Kilbride
These are the united parishes on the Firth of Lorne including Oban and the Isle of Kerrera. The Games are customarily held in Oban in early July in the Balinoe Field, Kilmore, from 11.00 to 17.00.

Kinlochleven
Seven miles east of Ballachulish, on the Inverness-shire–Argyll border, this is an 'aluminium' village built for the workers in the industry at the head of Loch Leven. The Games are usually held in early July on Island Park, an isthmus at the head of the loch, with the hills rising steeply above it on the other three sides.

Lairg
A small village in Sutherland on the River Shin, nine miles north of Bonar Bridge. A natural meeting place where all the roads converge, it is the centre for the Lairg Highland Sheep Sales when there are usually something like 30,000 Cheviot lambs for sale. Another combination of a Games and an agricultural show, but this time in a Highland setting, the Games are held after the Lairg Crofters' Agricultural Show, usually towards the end of August.

Langholm
A small, attractive, old grey Border town on the River Esk, Langholm is essentially a mill town manufacturing tweed, notable for its Common Riding celebrations. Like Galashiels and Selkirk

the Games which follow sometimes include Highland dancing and other Highland Games events.
The Common Riding is usually held in late July.

Lesmahagow
A sizeable Lanarkshire town some five miles
south-west of Lanark, these Amateur Games are
currently held in mid-June.

Lochboisdale
A small village on South Uist. The Games are
generally held early in July, on the Askernish
Machair and a feature is the solo piping. They
are timed to tie in with the Lochmaddy Games
in North Uist. (*See below*)

Lochearnhead
The Balquhidder, Lochearnhead and Strathyre
Highland Games are held in Lochearnhead, a
small village strategically placed at the head of
Loch Earn ten miles north of Callander, generally
in mid-August. These Games originated in the
1880s but were never very notable until Ewan
Cameron, Scottish heavyweight champion in 1953
and owner of the Lochearnhead Hotel, took over
as Secretary in 1949. Backed by a hard-working
committee, the Games became a major event.

Lochinver
This is a small fishing village and popular tourist resort on Loch Inver on the west coast of
Sutherland, particularly geared to climbers in the
surrounding mountains and to fishermen attracted
to the many small lochs in the area. The port presents a charming, almost Mediterranean, picture
from a distance on a sunny day. The Assynt

Gathering is generally held in the An Culag Park in early August. The chieftain arrives in a decorated fishing boat to be greeted by a pipe band on the quayside and escorted to the park to perform the opening ceremony. An unusual feature of these Games is the long distance fly-casting competition.

Loch Lomond
See Balloch

Lochmaddy
This North Uist village on the sea loch of the same name usually holds its annual Games early in July in the lee of the sand dunes on the Sollas Machair to get the maximum shelter from the Atlantic winds. When really blowing a gale, it can be readily understood that this can have a considerable effect on the performances of all concerned.

Lonach
Held towards the end of August in Bellabeg Park in Upper Donside, eleven miles north of Ballater in Aberdeenshire, the Lonach Gathering dates from 1822, when it was decided to form 'The Lonach Highland and Friendly Society' with the aims, among others, of the 'preservation of the Highland Dress'. A prominent feature of the Gathering is the 'March of the Clansmen', when the Forbes, Gordons and Wallaces march six miles round the great houses of the district armed with pikes, broadswords and halberds before arriving at the ground to march past at the Games. This has been frequently copied in the USA. The piping starts from 09.30 onwards and all other events from 13.00 to 17.00. Advance booking is necessary.

Luss
A small tourist village on the west side of Loch
Lomond, eleven miles north of Dumbarton, Luss
is particularly well placed with fine views over
the loch towards the slopes of Ben Lomond. The
Games were first started in 1926 on land owned by
the Colquhouns of Luss, where they are still held,
generally in mid-July. Notable features are the hill
race and the size of the caber, which is always too
large to toss at the start and is sawn down until it
can be thrown.

Mallaig
Mallaig is a thriving village and fishing port, forty-
one miles west of Fort William in Inverness-shire.
The Mallaig Games caused so many traffic jams
on the narrow but picturesque road approaching
Mallaig that they had to be moved to Morar three
miles to the south and are now officially the
Mallaig and Morar Games. They are usually held
in early August in Beoraid Park on the shores of
Loch Morar, to reach which one passes close by
the River Morar, the shortest river in Scotland at
less than half a mile in length from loch to sea.
The Game's chieftain is Lord Lovat. The Games
usually start at 12.00 and continue until 17.00.

Markinch
A small town in mid-Fife, now greatly over-
shadowed by its very much larger New Town
neighbour Glenrothes, Markinch is notable principally for its well-known grain-whisky distillery
owned by Haig. The Games originated in the 1920s
and though suspended in 1973 were re-started in
1974. They are generally held in early June in the
Dixon Park in the middle of the town; a feature of
the Games is the pipe band competition.

Montrose

At the mouth of the River Esk, this small port and rather sleepy royal burgh in north-east Angus is an attractive place to visit. The Games are generally held in early August and feature the usual local and open events. The local events usually start at 10.00 and the open events at 13.00.

Mull

See Tobermory

Nairn

This attractive small county town and municipal burgh on the Moray Firth is fifteen miles east of Inverness. The Amateur Games are generally held in mid-August and are usually well attended.

Nethy Bridge

See Abernethy

Newburgh

This small royal burgh with a harbour lies on the south side of the Firth of Tay, eight miles north-west of Cupar. Until 1850 the Games consisted of a pony race from the West Port out on the Abernethy road. After 1850 this was altered to a coble race on the River Tay. This race remains a special and unique feature of the modern Highland Games with four heats and over sixty boats taking part. The Games are generally held around mid-June in the Mugdrum Park from 12.30 to 17.30.

Newtonmore

A small village in central Inverness-shire in the Spey Valley, Newtonmore is geared to visitors for climbing, pony trekking, and skiing. It is only three miles south of its rather larger and more prosperous rival Kingussie. Each has a keen shinty team and matches are fiercely contested. The Amateur Games, usually held in early August, include the North of Scotland Putt Championship and also the Clan Macpherson Gathering.

Oban

This is a well-known west-coast seaport, municipal burgh and tourist centre in Argyll, opposite the Island of Mull on the Firth of Lorne. The Argyllshire Gathering, with the Duke of Argyll as chieftain, is customarily held towards the end of August in its own field with a grandstand outside the town. These Games were first started in 1871 and have flourished ever since, possibly because they are valued as the considerable tourist attraction they undoubtedly are. They generally begin at 11.00 and go on to 16.15.

Oldmeldrum

This attractive small Aberdeenshire village four miles north of Inverurie consists largely of a central square, well served with inns. It is perhaps chiefly notable for its nearby malt whisky distillery, making the very good malt whisky Glengarioch (pronounced Glengeerie) and for its TV station. The Meldrum Sports, held in pleasant parkland, provide a varied programme which includes the North of Scotland Pipe Major Competition. The sports are usually held in the early part of June in the Pleasure Park, Oldmeldrum, from 11.00 to 18.00 on the Saturday and 12.00 onwards on the Sunday.

Paisley

South-west of Glasgow and now virtually indistinguishable from it, Paisley generally holds these popular and well-organised Amateur Games towards the end of July.

Peebles

Peebles, an attractive Border town on the upper reaches of the Tweed in a lovely setting well accustomed to tourists, usually holds its pleasant small Games early in September on a good site in the Tweed Valley. They sometimes include heavy events and a pipe band competition, but recently only Highland dancing. Starting at 13.00 they continue to 17.00.

Perth

The capital of Perthshire and the Gateway to the Highlands, Perth is well placed on the broad reaches of the River Tay, which flows through the town. The Games are customarily held on the South Inch towards mid-August from 12.30 to 17.00 and special features are the 90 metres Scottish Sprint Championship and the 1,000 metres Scottish Cycle Championship.

Peterhead

A municipal burgh and developing seaport in the district of Buchan in north-east Aberdeenshire, twenty-eight miles north of Aberdeen itself, Peterhead stands on a promontory and is widely known for the large state prison which broods forbiddingly one mile south of the town. The Games were started in 1962 and are generally held towards the end of July, being chiefly notable for the originality of the features presented.

Pitlochry

This well-known tourist centre in the south-eastern Highlands, twenty-four miles north of

Perth, is beautifully placed in the Tummel Valley. Held in the Recreation Ground, they are usually held in September amongst the last of the Games.

Rosneath and Clynder
Two neighbouring villages in Dunbartonshire on the west side of the Gare Loch on the promontory bordered on the east by Loch Long, these Highland Games include open heavy events and cycling. They are are generally held on a Sunday in mid-July in the Howie Park, Rosneath.

Rothesay
A royal burgh and the county town of the Isle of Bute, situated fourteen miles south-west of Greenock on the Firth of Clyde, this is very a popular summer coastal resort and yachting centre. These are Amateur Games, but the meeting counts towards the Champion of Champions League for pipe bands and attracts the very best as a result. They are usually held around mid-August from 12.00 to 17.30.

St Andrews
This well-known golfing Mecca and university town on the east coast of Fife between Leuchars and Crail attracts large numbers of visitors. The Games are usually held near the end of July from 13.00 to 17.00.

Selkirk
A thriving Border county town, like Galashiels it holds an annual Common Riding of the boundaries with a ceremony at the old market cross, attended by many expatriates. Like Galashiels and

Langholm the Games which follow sometimes feature Highland dancing and other Highland Games events. The Common Riding is usually held in mid-June.

Shotts
This quite large Lanarkshire mining town lies six miles north of Wishaw and has always had a particular character of its own. These are Amateur Games, but this is another of the five competitions counting towards the Champion of Champions League so it attracts all the best pipe bands. The Games are currently held early in June.

Skye
Skye is one of the largest and perhaps the best known of all the Inner Hebridean Islands, shortly to be joined to the mainland by a bridge. The Isle of Skye Games were started in 1878 and are usually held in the capital, Portree, in probably one of the most picturesque settings in Scotland: overlooking the harbour with the magnificent Cuillins in the background. The field is small, but the spectators are well placed above it. They are generally held in the latter half of August from 10.00 to 17.00.

Southend
At the extreme end of the Kintyre peninsula eight miles south of Campbeltown this small village is geared to tourism. These small Games are usually held towards the end of July, starting at 18.00 and continuing to 21.30.

Stonehaven
This attractive old seaport and county town of Kincardineshire fourteen miles south of Aberdeen

holds its annual Games in the Mineralwell Park, generally towards mid-July from 11.00 to 17.00.

Stranraer
This seaport at the head of Loch Ryan in Wigtownshire five miles north of Portpatrick is the site of the ferry service to Ireland. The Galloway Games are held in the London Road Playing Fields and feature the European Heavy Events Open Championships. They are usually held in early August, starting at 11.30 and continuing to 17.30.

Strathmiglo
This small village in north-west Fife holds its annual Games in early June at the King George V Playing Field, generally starting at 12.30 and ending at 17.30.

Strathpeffer
This Victorian spa, once particularly noted for its mineral springs, lies five miles west of Dingwall, the county town, and still retains considerable popularity as a holiday resort. The Games are held in the grounds of Leod Castle, with the mountains towering above them. Started in 1881 by carpenters working at the spa, they have continued ever since. A date prior to the shooting season is chosen to avoid a clash of interests, for Strathpeffer is surrounded by particularly beautiful grouse moor and deerstalking country. Usually held on the Saturday before 12 August from 11.00 to 16.30.

Taynuilt
Nine miles east of Oban on the south shore of Loch Etive, this is a small Highland village geared to tourism. The Games are held towards

the end of July in the sports field, usually from 13.00 to 17.00.

Thornton
This comparatively small town four miles north of Kirkcaldy in Fife has organised Highland Games since 1864. Generally held early in July in the Memorial Park, particular features are pony trotting and cycling as well as a dog show. They usually start at 13.00 and end at 17.30.

Thurso
The northernmost town in Caithness, eighteen miles north of Wick, Thurso is the atomic capital of the north with its giant golfball-shaped experimental atomic reactor at nearby Dounreay. The Games, like the Halkirk Games, also claim the title of the Caithness Highland Games, and were started in the early 1970s under the chieftainship of Lord Thurso. Currently held in early July in the Millbank Park they (along with Durness further to the west) are the northernmost on the mainland of Scotland and feature a contest for the Heavyweight Championship of the Highlands. They are generally held from 13.00 to 17.30.

Tobermory
This well-known seaport on the attractive Isle of Mull faces the Sound of Mull and lies seven miles north-west of Oban with a regular ferry service to the mainland. The Games were started in 1926 and are generally held around mid-July on Tobermory golf course with the spectators seated on a steep bank overlooking the Sound of Mull, able to see as far as the Morvern Hills on the mainland on a clear day. Such a fine natural setting must be hard to beat anywhere in Scotland. Lord McLean

of Duart is the chieftain. The Games usually start
at 11.00 and end at 16.30.

Tomintoul

One of the highest villages in Scotland, Tomintoul
lies twelve miles south of Ballindalloch in Banffshire. Close to the wild Glenlivet area, where illegal
whisky distilling was once rife and where some
of the finest whisky in Scotland is still produced,
this is a village well used to tourists. The Games
are amongst the oldest as well being the highest,
although no longer held in the large village square,
but more suitably today in a clearing outside the
village. They are traditionally held on the third Saturday in July and 1992 will be the 150th Games.

The Highland Games Overseas

Highland Games enthusiasts will see from the survey below that they are to be found almost anywhere throughout the world. It will be appreciated that the organisers of many Highland Games tend to change annually, hence addresses tend to become out of date very quickly. Where possible useful back-up addresses have been provided, but application to the local Chamber of Commerce, or Tourist Board, will usually provide further details should these sources fail. In general it may be assumed that the normal piping, dancing and heavy events are included in the day with, as far as possible, any unusual events also mentioned.

ASIA

HONG KONG
The St Andrew's Society holds periodic Highland Games and since 1987 annual Pipe Band Championships. These take place at Stanley Fort and are usually sponsored by a well-known Scotch whisky firm. *Contact*: HK St Andrew's Society, c/o Lowe, Bingham and Matthews, Princes Building, Hong Kong.

INDONESIA

Jakarta Highland Gathering
Founded in 1975, this is usually held about one month after the end of Ramadan. In 1990 the sixteenth Gathering was held on 3 June. Piping,

Dancing, heavy and track events are all held, also volley-ball, tug-of-war, seven-a-side rugby. Special events may include wood-chopping, parachuting. The main Scottish event is Open Quintet for invited pipe bands consisting of three pipers, one bass drummer and one side drummer. Bands come from Australia, New Zealand, Hong Kong, Malaysia, Singapore, Japan and Scotland, also in 1990 one from France. A special Quintet competition is restricted to SE Asian indigenous players. Finale of massed bands, attended by four to five thousand spectators, seventy per cent of whom are Indonesian. *Contact*: A. Macfarlane, c/o Lemigas, PO Box 89/JKT, Cipulir, Kebayoran Lama, Jakarta 1002, Indonesia *Fax* 62 21 716150.

AUSTRALASIA

AUSTRALIA
Games are held regularly at Bundanoon, Campbell-town, Penrith and Sydney in NSW and at Ross, Tasmania and Ringwood, Victoria. In addition there are many Games held periodically. Unfortunately many now seem to have varying dates and venues, while some are restricted solely to piping and dancing. The following list gives details of some of the best known Games, followed by addresses of organisations which may be able to provide helpful information about Highland Games in their area.

NEW SOUTH WALES
Sydney Highland Games
Founded in 1856 these are by far the oldest and largest Highland Games in Australia and are held annually on New Year's Day. They include massed pipe bands, heavy events, athletic events, Highland dancing, and individual piping, also clan

tents and numerous other attractions. They have an annual spectator attendance of over fifteen thousand.

Useful Addresses

Australasian Highlander
Mrs Colleen McEwan, PO Box 210, Charleston, NSW 2290.
Monaro Caledonian Society
Contact: Denis Wilmore, PO Box 339, Cooma North, NSW 2630.
The Scottish Australian Heritage Council
Contact: Gwen MacLennan, GPO Box 421, Sydney, NSW 2001.

QUEENSLAND
Queensland Pipe Band Association
Contact: Mr David Lyall, GPO Box 1218, Brisbane, Qld 4001.

SOUTH AUSTRALIA
Royal Caledonian Society of South Australia
Secretary: Reginald M. Verrall, 7 Warrego Crescent, Linden Park, SA 5065.
South Australia Pipe Band Association
Mr Lindsay Chuck, 18 Grazing Avenue, Morphett Vale, SA 5162.

TASMANIA
Ross Highland Games
Founded in 1958 and organised by the Tasmanian Caledonian Council, these Games are held annually on the second Saturday in March at Ross, a small historic town in the centre of Tasmania, between Launceston and Hobart. The Tasmanian Pipe Band Association conducts the pipe band contest. Solo piping and dancing and the usual heavy events are also included. Other features are dog training and clan tents.

Useful Addresses
Tasmanian Caledonian Council
Hon Secretary: Mrs D. Laverty, 425 West Tamar Road, Riverside, Tas 7250 *Tel*: 273180.
Tasmanian Caledonian Society
Founded 1920. *Hon Secretary*: Miss G. F. Nichols, 3 Benjafield Terrace, Mt Stuart, Tas 7000.
Tasmanian Pipe Band Association
Contact: Mr Rod McGee, 1 Calder Crescent, Blackman's Bay, Tas 7152.
Saint Andrew Society of Hobart
Founded 1960. *Secretary*: G. Livingstone, 13 McGuiness Crescent, Lenah Valley, Hobart, Tas 7008.

VICTORIA
City of Newtown Highland Gathering, Geelong
Founded in 1957 these Games are held in the splendid setting in Queen's Park, Geelong on the weekend following the second Monday in March with the main events on Sunday. They include pipe bands, Highland dancing, heavy events, also competitions for the best dressed lad and lassie, Scottish dog breeds and gumboot hurling.
Contact: David Smith, City Manager, City of Newtown, 263 Pakington St, Newton and PO Box 1250, Geelong 3220 *Tel*: (052) 22 1033.
Daylesford Highland Gathering
Founded in 1952 these Games are held in the fine setting of the Victoria Park in this well-known holiday spa town. Held originally on the first Saturday and Sunday in December, the main street of Daylesford is closed on Saturday for March of the Pipe Bands. Events include pipe bands, Highland dancing and heavy events.
Organising Secretary: Mrs Wendy Faulkhead, PO Box 36, Daylesford 3460, Victoria, Australia *Tel*: (053) 48–3403.

Victoria Highland Pipe Band Association
Contact: Mrs Margaret Johnston, PO Box 283, Box
Hill, Vic 3128.

WESTERN AUSTRALIA
Western Pipe Band Association
Contact: Mr Digby Claydon, 1/10 McLean Street,
Melville, WA 6156.

NEW ZEALAND

In both North Island and South Island it goes
without saying that the various games are held
in surroundings very reminiscent of the Scottish
Highlands and the participants are commonly
descended from original settlers, in many cases
from Nova Scotia. Several shiploads, for example,
came from there to Waipu with the Rev Norman
McLeod in the early 1850s.

NORTH ISLAND
As late as the 1960s many more Highland Games
were held regularly on North Island than take
place today – at Marton, Wanganui, Feilding
and Masterton for example, to name only a
few. Some of these still hold dancing and/or
piping competitions, so that it is worth making
local enquiries. Games are still held regularly at
the following locations.
Auckland Highland Games
Founded in 1977 these Games are held in Auckland
usually on the Saturday nearest to St Andrew's Day.
They include particularly pipe bands, Highland
dancing and piping as well as the usual heavy
events.
Secretary: Mrs Tina Robertson , 19 Larnoch Road,
Henderson, Auckland.

Hastings Highland Games

Founded in 1950 they are held annually on the Saturday and Sunday before Easter and include pipe bands, heavy events, dancing, piping and drumming, also wood-chopping, athletics, tug-of-war, and tossing the gumboot.

Contact: K. McMillan, 34 Scott Drive, Havelock North.

Palmerston North Highland Gathering

Held on the second Saturday in December these Games are officially known as Square Day as the Gathering is held in the City Square. They include piping, dancing and a pipe band contest, as well as sometimes haggis hurling.

Contact: Mrs Jenny Mair, 9 Glen Street, Palmerston North.

Tauranga Highland Games

These Games are generally held bi-annually on the third weekend in March, but it has been irregular. In 1990 there was a successful two-day meeting, the largest ever held in New Zealand, with competitions of every conceivable nature.

Contact: David Bean, 4 Cameron Rd, Tauranga.

Turakina Highland Games

Founded in 1865 these Games are generally held on the last Saturday in January. Organised by the Turakina Caledonian Society they claim to be the oldest Games in New Zealand (*but see* Waipu *below*). They include piping, dancing, a pipe band contest, Scottish field events and tossing the gumboot.

Secretary: Don J. Fitchet, 56A Fox Road, Wanganui.

Waipu Annual Highland Games

Started by the earliest settlers from Skye who arrived via Nova Scotia in 1853 with Dr Norman McLeod. The Games were officially founded in 1871 and are the oldest in New Zealand. Organised by the Waipu Caledonian Society, they are always held on 1 January except when it falls on a Sunday. The Games include piping, dancing and the usual heavy events, as well as sheaf throwing, stone carrying and weight carrying.

Secretary: Mrs J. Baxter, c/o Picketts, Police Station, Waipu *Tel*: (089) 432–0210.

SOUTH ISLAND

Hamilton Highland Games

Founded in 1984 these Games are usually held on 31 December in the Fairlie Showgrounds, sixty-two kilometres west of Timaru. They include piping, dancing, caber tossing, tug-of-war and a hill race, with a special prize for the highest awards in the piping, caber tossing and hill race. In event of a tie, the best performer of the Highland Fling to win. Piano smashing, wood-chopping and a rooster race are also included.

Contact: Mr R. Shand, PO Box 13, Fairlie.

Mackenzie Highland Show

Held at Fairlie and run by the Mackenzie County Agricultural and Pastoral Society. Piping and dancing are features, but there are no other Highland events. Wood chopping, horse and pony events are also included.

Secretary: Mrs A. Bell, Hillcrest, 17 RD, Fairlie.

South Canterbury Caledonian Games

Founded in 1875 and organised by the South Canterbury Caledonian Society, the 115th Games were held in 1990. They are held annually on 1 January in the Caledonian Grounds and concentrate on Highland dancing and piping, with amateur athletics, cycling events and wood chopping.

Secretary: Mr M. Thin, Langridge Road, Temuka.

Temuka Caledonian Games

Founded 103 years ago in 1887 and usually held on 2 January, these Games include Highland dancing and piping, also amateur athletics and amateur and professional cycling.

Secretary: Mrs R. Hix, PO Box 116, Temuka.

Waimate Caledonian Society Games

Founded in 1875, the 115th meeting was held at Victoria Park in 1990. Highland dancing and piping are the only Highland events, but athletics and cycling events are also included.

Secretary: Mrs W. Todd, 31 Rugby Street, Waimate.

Useful Addresses

Piping and Dancing Association of New Zealand

Contact: P and D A, c/o South Canterbury Centre, Timaru.

St Andrew's Scottish Society Inc (Southlands)

Founded 1915.

Hon Secretary: G.M. McLennan, PO Box 1236, Invercargill, Southland.

NORTH AMERICA

CANADA

With so many settlers from Scotland, it is not surprising that very many Highland Games and Festivals are held in Canada throughout the summer months. Each of the provinces has at least one, with a particular abundance in Ontario, about which information is most readily available. Nova Scotia also takes great pride in its Scottish heritage and has held a grand 'International Gathering of the Clans' on several occasions during the summer tourist season. Where information is limited concerning any particular Games, the local Tourist Board should be able to provide further details. In overall charge of the Canadian Highland Games is:

The Canadian Highland Games Council, 63 Brant Avenue, Brantford, Ontario N3T 3H2 *Tel*: (519) 753–5027.

Calgary Highland Games
These Games were founded in 1976 and are held in Calgary.
Red Deer Highland Games
Held annually in Red Deer.

Manitoba Highland Gathering or
Selkirk Gathering
Founded in 1966 and known as 'Western Canada's Finest Gathering' these Games are generally held on the first Saturday in July in Selkirk Park on the Red River in the town of Selkirk, just north of Winnipeg. The Games include piping, dancing and heavy events, also sheepdog work, sheep-shearing, York-boat (the traditional Red River heavy transport boat propelled by oars and sail) racing on the Red River as well as a Highland cattle display. Clan gathering participation.
Contact: Don Porter, Box 59, Selkirk, Manitoba, R1A 2B1 *Tel*: 482–5726.

New Brunswick Highland Games
Founded in 1980 these Games usually take place on the last weekend in June at the Waasis Road Sports Field, Oromocto.
Contact: The New Brunswick Tourist Board.

Nova Scotia's International Gathering of the Clans is held every four years. The 1991 Gathering was selected as the most popular tourist event in Canada by the American Bus Association. Each of the following Games is included among the events of the Gathering, which last throughout the summer.

Useful Addresses:

The Clansman

Describing itself as 'an ethnic journal' the *Clansman* is published six times a year. It contains information and news about the Scottish events held in Nova Scotia.

Contact: Clansman Publishing, PO Box 8805, Station A, Halifax, Nova Scotia B3K 5M4 *Tel:* 902 452 9263 *Fax*: 902 454 4600 *Games*

Annapolis Valley Highland Games

The Annapolis Valley lays claim to the first landing of Scots in North America in 1598 and the first settlement of Scots in 1629. The Games were founded in 1987 by the Annapolis Valley Highland Society because of the large number of people of Scottish descent living in the area. They are held annually on the last Saturday in August in the town of Middleton on the former race track area. The Games include pipe band and heavy event championships, Highland dancing and piping, a Highland hill run of eight miles, a kilted golf tournament and a ceilidh.

Antigonish Highland Games

Founded in 1863 and claiming to be 'the oldest Scottish festival in North America' the Games are held each July in Antigonish 'the Highland heart of Nova Scotia.' The Antigonish Highland Games Week, one of Nova Scotia's great tourist attractions, generally starts on the first Saturday in July with children's events, a Highland Ball and social events. Since 1948 the Games themselves have taken place over three days on an attractive site at Columbus from the Friday over the second weekend in July. The Games include the usual heavy and track events, a pipe band competition, Highland dancing, solo piping and drumming, also a kilted golf tournament and a 10,000 metre race. They are closely associated with the St Francis Xavier University, which has an extensive collection of Celtic works.

Contact: St Francis Xavier University, Box 80, Antigonish, Nova Scotia B2G 1C0 *Tel*: 902 867 2473.

Metro Scottish Festival and Highland Games

These Games are held in the Wanderer's Grounds in Halifax. They last two days over the first weekend in July.

Contact: The North British Society, PO Box 5125, Station A, Halifax, Nova Scotia B3L 4M7.

ONTARIO

Useful Addresses

4th Battalion Royal Canadian Regiment, Pipe Band *Contact*: Pipe Major Ralph F. Haddral CD, 291 Hibernia St, Stratford, Ont. N5A 5V9.

Clans and Scottish Societies of Canada

Contact: 95 Laurel Avenue, Etobicoke *Tel*: 416 234 0062.

Dancers Association of Ontario

Secretary: Mrs Olive N. Fraser, 53 Aberdeen Rd, S Cambridge, Ont N16 2X6.

Scottish Banner

Describing itself as 'the largest Scottish newspaper in the world outside Scotland' the *Scottish Banner* contains information about news and events in the Scottish community, including an annual list of Highland Games held throughout North America.

Contact: the *Scottish Banner*, Box 200, Station H, Toronto, Ont M4C 5J2 *Tel*: 416 469 3939 *Fax*: 416 469 3913.

Sons of Scotland Benevolent Association

Contact: 90 Eglinton Avenue E, Toronto, Ont M5H 1Y9 *Tel*: 416 482 1250.

Cambridge Highland Games

These Games are generally held in Churchill Park on the third Saturday in July and include the Ontario Open Highland Dance Championships.

Cobourg Highland Games

On the shore of Lake Ontario, one hour's drive from Toronto, the town of Cobourg usually holds these Games each year in Donegan Park on the first Saturday in July.

Dutton Highland Games

These Games are generally held in the Sons of Scotland Park on the second Saturday in June.

Fergus Highland Games and Scottish Festival

Founded in 1946 these Games are held in the town of Fergus, some ten miles north-west of Guelph. Fergus itself was established in 1833 by two Scots, Adam Ferguson and James Webster, and the Scottish influence continued for many years. This is claimed to be the largest Highland Festival in North America and is generally held on the second weekend in August in the Victoria Park, designed to look like Braemar in Scotland. A tattoo is held on the preceding Friday. Important features of the Games are the International and North American Scottish Heavy Events Championships and North American Tug-of-War Championships. The Games also include pipe bands, solo piping and Highland dancing.

Georgetown Highland Games

Founded in 1975 and originally known as the Halton Hills Highland Games and Festival, these are generally held on the third Saturday in June in the Georgetown Fairgrounds. They include pipe band competitions, Highland dancing and piping, and heavy events.

Contact: Chamber of Commerce, PO Box 111, Georgetown, Ont L7G 4T1 *Tel*: 416 877 7119.

Georgina Highland Games

These small Games are held in Keswick, a town near the southern tip of Lake Simco. They are usually held in the Keswick Arena on the third Saturday in June and include pipe bands, Highland dancing and heavy events.

Glengarry Highland Games

Founded in 1948, these Games are generally held in the Agricultural Grounds of Maxville, Ontario on the Saturday before the first Monday in August. They claim to be the world's largest Games and never rained off in forty-three years. A pre-Games grandstand show with a concert, tattoo and displays takes place on the Friday evening. Notable features include the North American Pipe Band Championship, drum majors competitions, piping and Highland dancing, as well as track and field events.

Haliburton Highland Games

Located in the scenic 'cottage country' several hours to the north of Toronto, Haliburton generally holds its annual Games in the Glebe Park on the fourth Saturday in June.

Contact: Haliburton Highland Games, PO Box 29, Haliburton, Ont KoM 1So *Tel*: 705 457 3555.

Molson Highland Games

Founded in 1985 these Games are usually held each year on the fourth Saturday in July at Molson Park, Barrie, which is capable of coping with over 30,000 spectators comfortably. They include pipe bands, solo piping and dancing, also the usual heavy events, as well as 'The Farmer's Walk' in which competitors have to carry 200 pounds in each hand for as far as they can. These Games already claim to be amongst the largest three Highland Games in Ontario.

North Lanark Highland Games

Founded in 1984 these Games are held annually on the fourth Saturday in August in the Fairgrounds of the North Lanark Agricultural Society on the banks of the Mississippi River. There are the usual piping, dancing and heavy events included in the day's programme.

Sarnia Highland Games

Usually held on the third Saturday in August in the Centennial Park, Sarnia, these games include the All-Ontario Heavy Events Championships, the North American Haggis Hurling Competition, and a sheepdog demonstration, as well as the usual events.

Sertoma Highland Games

Generally the first Games of the year to be held in Ontario, these usually take place on the holiday Saturday at the end of May.

TJ Shaughnessy Memorial Highland Games

These small Games are usually held in the historical Old Fort Erie in the town of Fort Erie towards the end of June.

Zorra Highland Games

These Games are generally held in the Matheson Park, Embro, on the first Saturday of July. They are not far to drive from the celebrated Stratford Theatre Festival.

PRINCE EDWARD ISLAND

Caledonian Club Highland Games

Held annually.
Contact: Prince Edward Island Tourist Board.

QUEBEC

Montreal Highland Games

These annual Games are usually held at St-Lambert

on the eastern side of the St Lawrence River during the first weekend of August.

UNITED STATES OF AMERICA

Numerous Games and Gatherings take place throughout the United States all through the year, often in conjunction with the annual meetings of Clan Societies. Dates, venues and even the names of the Games often change, and it is advisable to consult the local Chamber of Commerce, or the listings in the *Highlander* magazine or the *Scottish American* (*see below*) for the most up-to-date information. Games are listed in alphabetical order according to the state in which they are held.

Highlander
This magazine, with articles and news of Scottish interest, appears seven times a year. Each issue has a valuable listing of forthcoming events; the April issue contains a directory with a section devoted to forthcoming Highland Games.
Contact: *Highlander*, 202 S Cook St, Suited 214, PO Box 397, Barrington IL, 60011 *Tel*: 708 382 1035 *Fax*: 708 382 0322.

Scottish-American
Published bi-monthly 'for Lowlanders and Highlanders alike' this is also packed with articles and news of Scottish interest. Details of current Highland Games and Festivals are usually to be found in the appropriate issues.
Contact: *Scottish-American*, PO Box 4473, Star City, WV 26506 *Tel*: 304 599 1877 or 304 379 8803.

ALABAMA
Alabama Highland Games
Currently held at the Alabama Shakespeare Festival Grounds in Wynton Blount Cultural Park,

Montgomery, these Games usually take place on the third Saturday in September, with competitions in athletics, Highland dancing, solo piping and pipe bands, as well as numerous side-events including a Scottish fashion show and a Border Collie demonstration.

Contact: PO Box 6075, Montgomery, AL 36105

North Alabama Scottish Festival
Held in Sharon Johnstone Park, Huntsville at the end of April.

ALASKA

Alaskan Scottish Highland Games
Founded in 1982, these Games are usually held at Eagle River, Anchorage in late July or early August.

Contact: Alaskan Scottish Club, PO Box 3471, Anchorage, AK 99510.

ARIZONA

Arizona Highland Games
Founded in 1966 and generally held in Phoenix at the Tempe Diablo Soccer Field on the third Saturday in February.

Contact: David R. Logan, President, Caledonian Society of Arizona, 5219 S. 44th Pl, Phoenix, AZ 85040, or Donald C. Wlkinson, 4042 E Indianola Avenue, Phoenix, AZ 85018.

Tucson Highland Games
Generally held in mid-November.

Contact: PO Box 40665, Tucson, AZ 85715.

ARKANSAS

Ozark Scottish Festival
Founded in 1980 and organised by the Presbyterian College (itself founded 1872), the Games take place at the college in early April.

Contact: Arkansas College, Batesville, AR 72501.

CALIFORNIA

Caledonian Club of San Francisco Scottish Gathering and Games

Founded in 1966, the Games are generally held over the Labor Day weekend at Sonoma County Fairground, Santa Rosa, which holds over 30,000 spectators. The very tight schedule includes fiddling and the US Caber Championships.

Contact: John Dickson, Caledonian Club of San Francisco, 13210 Merced St, Richmond, CA 94804.

Campbell Highland Games

Founded in 1979, the Games currently take place in mid-October in Campbell, a town which developed from the ranch bought by Ben Campbell in 1881.

Contact: Campbell Chamber of Commerce, 328 E Campbell Avenue, Campbell, CA 95008.

Central Coast Gathering and Games

These Games are usually held in El Chorro Regional Park, San Luis Obispo on the first Saturday in May.

Contact: PO Box 13954, San Luis Obispo, CA 93406.

Fresno Highland Gathering and Games

Founded in 1978, the Fresno Games are generally held on a beautiful site on Coombs River Ranch in mid-September.

Marin County Highland Gathering

Founded in 1974, these Games usually take place at Marin County Day School in Corte Madera around mid-May.

Modesto Highland Games and Gathering

Founded in 1982, the Games are held on the first Saturday in June in the Tuolumne River Regional Park.

Contact: St Andrew's Society of Modesto, PO Box 2545, Modesto, CA 95351.

Monterey Highland Games
Founded in 1970 and generally held on the first Saturday in August at the Monterey Fairgrounds. *Contact*: Scottish Society of Monterey Peninsula, PO Box 1633, Carmel, CA 93921.

Pacific Highland Clan Gathering and Games
Founded in 1979 and currently held at San Bernadino County Junior Fairgrounds in Chino during the first weekend in October. *Contact*: John MacRae, President, Clans of Highlands Inc, 2308 Shady Hills Drive, Diamond Bar, CA 91765.

Sacramento Valley Scottish Games
Presently held in the Fairgrounds at Dixon on the third weekend in April.

San Diego Scottish Games
San Diego is Edinburgh's sister city and these Games, founded in 1974, are currently held in the Rancho Santa Fe Park on the second Saturday in June.

United Scottish Society's Highland Gathering and Games
Founded in 1927 and the fourth-oldest of the present Games, these are customarily held in the Orange County Fairground over the Memorial Day Weekend.

Yuba/Sutter Scottish Highland Games and Festival
These Games are currently held in the Riverfront Park Amphitheater at Marysville in mid-May.

COLORADO

Aurora Scottish Games
Founded in 1983, these Games are usually held on the third Saturday in May.

Long's Peak Scottish Highland Festival
Founded in 1978, these Games take place in Estes Park beside Lake Estes, a setting dominated by

Long's Peak (14,256 ft) The Games are customarily held over the first weekend after Labor Day.
Contact: PO Box 1820, Estes Park, CO 80517.
Pike's Peak Highland Games and Celtic Festival
Founded in 1983, the Games are currently held on the third Saturday in July at the Western Sportsman Association's Monument Lake Resort in Monument.
Rocky Mountain Highland Games
Founded in 1963, they are presently held in the Highland Heritage Park in Denver over two days during the second weekend in August and include an exhibition of Scottish cattle. The Sword of the Rockies is awarded for best Sword Dance.
Contact: S Andrews Society, c/o Charles Todd, 3606 E Hindsdale Pk, Littleton, CO 80122 *or* 911 W Belmont Place, Littleton, CO 80123.

CONNECTICUT
Round Hill Highland Games
First organised in 1923 these are the third oldest of the current Games. Sometimes termed the Cowal Games of the US, they usually take place in Cranberry Park on 4 July and include eleven-a-side soccer.
Contact: PO Box 261, Belden Station, Norwalk, CT 06850.
Scotland Highland Festival
Presently held at the Waldo Homestead, Scotland in early October.
St Andrew's Society of Connecticut
Scottish Festival
Founded in 1984, these Games are currently held at the Fairgrounds, Goshen, during the second weekend in October.
Contact: St Andrew's Society of Connecticut, PO Box 1195, Litchfield, CT 06759.

Dunedin Highland Games and Festival
Founded in 1966. Dunedin, the sister city to Stirling, is very conscious of its Scottish origins and the schools have pipe bands. The festivities last a week and include a tattoo, a Scottish concert and a golf tournament. The Games generally take place at Highlander Park in late March or early April and include a parade of tartans and a kilted mile. Many Canadians come south for these Games.

Contact: Dunedin Highland Games and Festival Committee, Inc PO Box 507, Dunedin FL 33528–0507.

Jacksonville Scottish Highland Games and Gathering of Clans
Founded in 1979 and currently held during the second weekend in April, the Games include a haggis hurl, medieval events and bonniest knees with blindfold judges and the release of racing pigeons as a Scottish sport.

Orlando Scottish Highland Games
Founded in 1978, these are notable as the first Games of the year in the USA and the third-largest in the South presently held at the Central Florida Fairgrounds during the second weekend in January with a ceilidh and whisky tasting on the Friday and a golf tournament on the Sunday, the Games themselves take place on the Saturday and include a haggis hurl and a sheepdog demonstration. They had a kilted sky-diver on one occasion. Visitors are encouraged to 'bring your kilt and swim suit'!

Contact: Orlando Scottish Highland Games, PO Box 300377, Fern Park, FL 32730 *Tel*: 407 339 3335.

Pensacola Highland Games
Currently held on a Saturday in mid-November.

South-East Florida Scottish Festival
Founded in 1984 and currently held at Crandon Gardens, Key Biscayne on the first Saturday in

March. Features include an eighteenth-century military encampment.

Contact: Scottish American Society of South Florida, PO Box 633, Miami Shores FL 33158.

Treasure Island Scottish Games

These Games are at present held in Treasure Island Community Park over the second weekend in November.

GEORGIA

Atlanta Celtic Festival

Currently held at Oglethorpe University at the end of April.

Savannah Scottish Highland Games

Founded in 1978 these Games are usually held on the first Saturday in May in Old Fort Jackson (built in 1809).

Contact: Savannnah Scottish Games Inc, PO Box 13435, Savannah, GA 31416.

Shellman Georgia Highland Games

These Games are currently held over the third weekend in November.

Contact: PO Box 532, Shellman, GA 30324.

Stone Mountain Scottish Festival and Highland Games

Founded in 1973, these Games are held over two days usually in mid-October at the foot of Stone Mountain, an 825-foot granite monolith. They include clan challenge athletics and a sheepdog demonstration.

Contact: PO Box 14023, Atlanta, GA 30324.

HAWAII

Honolulu Highland Games

Founded in 1982 and currently held on the first Saturday in April at Kuroda Field, Fort de Russy, the Games include lawn bowling and spear throwing.

Contact: Hawaiian Scottish Association, 2615 S King St, Suite 206, Honolulu HI 96826.

ILLINOIS
Chicago Scottish Festival
Currently held on the third Saturday and Sunday in October.
Contact: 26 E Atteridge Rd, Lake Forest, IL 60045.
Illinois St Andrew Society Highland Games
Currently held on the campus of the Chicago College of Osteopathic Medicine on the second Saturday in June.

INDIANA
Indiana Highland Games
These games are usually held on the second Saturday in July at the Zollner Stadium, Fort Wayne and include competitions in Highland dancing, solo pipe and drum. Other features are massed bands, athletics, country dancing and Border Collies.
Contact: Indiana Highland Games Inc, 7020 Salge Drive, Fort Wayne, IN 46835 *Tel*: 219 486 2658.
Orak Shrine Highland Games
Usually held in Michigan City in late August.

KENTUCKY
Glasgow Highland Games
Founded in 1986, these Games are generally held over the last weekend in May at the Barren River State Resort Park; 'the Family Fun Games' are part of a full weekend of Scottish-related festivities, including a tattoo, ceilidhs, a tartan ball, and a Scottish country dance. The Games themselves include the usual Highland events, a five–mile run and numerous side-shows.
Contact: 121 1/2 E Main St, PO Box 373, Glasgow, KY 42142 *Tel*: 502 651 3141.

Kentucky Scottish Weekend
Founded in 1983 these Games currently take place in General Butler State Resort Park in Carrolton over the second weekend in May, and include competitions in solo piping and drumming, pipe bands, Highland dancing, and amateur athletics. *Contact*: Kentucky Scottish Weekend, PO Box 91683, Louisville, KY 40291–0683 *or* Department of Parks, Frankfort, KY 40601.

MAINE
Maine Highland Games
Founded 1979, the Games are currently held at Thomas Point Beach, Brunswick, in mid-August and include Highland dancing, piping, athletics, children's events, also demonstrations of Scottish country dancing, fiddling and sheepdog work. *Contact*: 298 York St, York, ME 03909.
Trenton Acadian Scottish Festival
Founded 1980 and generally held near Acadia National Park in the third weekend in July, the Games include a tomahawk event and sheepdog demonstration.

MARYLAND
Colonial Highland Gathering and International Open Sheep-dog Trials
Founded in 1960 and presently held over the third Friday and Saturday in May at the Maryland Department of Natural Resources Site at Fair Hill. The Games include a heptathlon, fiddling and a sheep to shawl contest. *Contact*: Colonial Highland Gathering, 20 Wakefield Drive, Newark, DE 19711.
McHenry Highland Festival
Founded in 1990 and currently held during the first weekend in June at the Garrett County Fairgrounds, these are indoor Games and include

piping, pipe bands and Highland dancing displays, athletics and numerous side-events, notably a military encampment, sheepdog demonstrations and a golf tournament.

Contact: Deep Creek Lake/Garrett County Promotion Council, Courthouse, Oakland, MD 21550 *Tel*: 301 334 1948.

National Capital Area Scottish Festival
Currently held at Rockville High School at the beginning of May.

South Maryland Festival and Gathering
Founded in 1979, these Games are customarily held on the last Saturday in April at the Jefferson Patteson Park and Museum in St Leonard. They include folk music, a kilted mile, and fiddling.

MASSACHUSETTS
Berkshire Indoor Highland Games
Founded in 1984 and presently held on the second Saturday in May, they include children's events.
Contact: PO Box 54, Pittsfield, MA 01201.

Massachusetts Highland Games
Currently held at Waltham High School on the third Saturday in June.

Shriner's Scottish Games
Usually held in mid-July.

Tam o'Shanter Highland Games
Presently held at Romuva Park, Brockton, on the first Saturday in June.
Contact: 200 Buckminster Drive, Norwood, MA 02062.

MICHIGAN
Alma Highland Festival and Games
Founded in 1968, the Games are customarily held over the last weekend in May at Alma College, which has its own pipe band. Alma calls itself 'Scotland USA' and because of its

position it attracts both US and Canadian entries. The Games include Pipe Band Championships, fiddling, soccer, a road run, a farmer's walk, a sheepdog demonstration and a crafts fair.

Contact: PO Box 506, Alma, MI 48801.

Detroit Highland Games

Founded in 1867 and the second oldest of the current Games in the USA, these are held on the first Saturday in August in eighty-three acre historic Fort Wayne on the Detroit River, directly across from Windsor, Canada. Pipe bands, solo piping and dancing and heavy events. Organised by the St Andrew's Society of Detroit with entirely volunteer support.

Contact: F. Michael Smith, PO Box 32291, Detroit, Michigan, 48232 *Tel*: (313) 832–1849 *or* Arthur Cheney, 11326 Mayfield, Livonia, MI 48150 *Tel*: 313 422 4864.

MINNESOTA

St Paul Scottish Country Fair

Founded in 1972 and currently held on the First Saturday in May in the grounds of Macalister College, which offers courses in piping and Highland dancing. Includes exhibitions of wares of local artists from Indian beads to paintings.

Contact: Madison Sheely, Macalister College, 1600 Grand Avenue, St Paul MN 55105.

MISSISSIPPI

Highlands and Islands Scottish Festival

Usually held at Hiller Park in Biloxi early in September.

Contact: PO Box 431, Biloxi, MS 39633.

Jackson Highland Games

Held currently on the first Saturday in November.

MISSOURI
Kansas City Highland Games
Founded in 1968 and currently held on the first weekend in June, these Games include amateur heavies and drumming.
Contact: Kansas City Highland Games, PO Box 112, Shawnee Mission, KS 66222.

MONTANA
Highland Games and Gathering
Currently held in Billings on the second Saturday in June.
Missoula Scottish Heritage Society Games
Currently held in Missoula on the second Saturday in August.

NEW HAMPSHIRE
Loon Mountain Highland Games
Founded in 1976, these Games aree held in the White Mountain National Forest at Loon Mt. Recreational Centre over three days of the weekend following Labor Day. They include Harp and Fiddle Championships, the Loon Mountain Stone Carry (240 lb), a kilted race and an eighteenth-century military encampment (74th Argyll Highlanders).
Contact: PO Box 130, Cambridge, MA 02238–0130.

NEW JERSEY
Bonnie Brae Scottish Games
These Games are currently held on the second Saturday in June.
Contact: Director of Development, Bonnie Brae, Millington, NJ 07946.

NEW MEXICO
Rio Grande Valley Celtic Festival and Highland Games
Currently held on the second Saturday in May at

the Menaul School in Albuquerque.

NEW YORK
Adirondack Scottish Games
Founded in 1977, these Games are currently held on the first Saturday in June at Crandall Park, Glen Falls.
Contact: Harold Kirkpatrick, 492 Glen St, Glen Falls, NY 121801.
Amherst Museum Scottish Festival
Customarily held at the Amherst Museum in mid-September.
Contact: Amherst Museum, Amherst, NY.
Capital District Highland Games
Founded in 1978, these Games are usually held in Altamont, a small town near Albany in a good rural setting, on the Saturday before Labor Day. The Games include a Scottie dog and bonniest knees contest.
Contact: 40 Terrace Avenue, Albany, NY 12203.
Central New York Scottish Games
Founded in 1934 these are the fifth-oldest of the current Games held in the USA. They are currently held on the second Saturday in August at Griffin Field on Lake Onondaga near Liverpool and are sponsored by the Clan Douglas.
Contact: Joseph Walker, 160 Stafford Avenue, Syracuse, NY 13206.
Long Island Scottish Games
Founded in 1961 these Games are usually held on the fourth Saturday in August on the lawn of old Westbury Mansion and Gardens.
Contact: Long Island Scottish Games, 30 Bluegrass Lane, Levittown, NY 11756 *Tel*: 516 883 9396.

NORTH CAROLINA
Flora Macdonald Highland Games.
Founded in 1977, these Games are usually held

at Red Springs on the first weekend in October. They include a re-enactment of Revolutionary War battles.

Contact: Flora Macdonald Highland Games Inc, PO Box 547, Red Springs, NC 28377.

Grandfather Mountain Highland Games and Gathering of Scottish Clans

Founded in 1956 and held in the superb setting of the MacRae Meadow at the foot of the Grandfather Mountain, this is one of the best known and now one of the largest Games in the USA, known as America's Braemar. The festivities start with a picnic and opening ceremony on Thursday and last four days over the first full weekend following 4 July. Clan meetings and social events take place on Friday, and the Games themselves follow on the Saturday and Sunday, including a parade of over 100 clans, as well as numerous traditional events. The Games are sponsored by Scottish Heritage USA Inc.

Contact: Cheryl Farthing, PO Box 356, Banner Elk, NC 28604. *Tel:* 704 898 5286.

Waxhaw Scottish Games

Founded in 1980, these Games are usually held on the last Saturday in October in a large natural outdoor theatre.

Contact: Scottish Society of the Waxhaws Ltd, Robert Burns Station, PO Box 143, Waxhaw, NC 28173.

OHIO

Ohio Scottish Games

Founded in 1978, the Games are customarily held at Oberlin College on the fourth Saturday in June. As well as the usual events they include rugby and a kilted mile.

Contact: Ohio Scottish Games, PO Box 21169, Cleveland, OH 44121.

OKLAHOMA
Highland Festival
Currently held at Rogers State College, Claremore on the third Saturday in April.
Oklahoma Scottish Games and Gathering
Founded in 1980 'The Friendly Games' are held in Mannion Park, Tulsa on the fourth Saturday in September. After a slow start, attendance figures now exceed 5,000. Events include pipe bands, solo piping, Highland dancing and tug-of-war, also includes amateur heavy events, a ladies haggis toss, and children's competitions.
Contact: Secretary Ruth Rankin, PO Box 9796, Tulsa, OK 74157–0796.

OREGON
Athena Caledonian Games
Founded in 1899 and re-started in 1976, the Games are currently held on the second Saturday in July. They include a women's caber and rolling-pin toss, a tattoo, and free beer for all spectators wearing the kilt. An added attraction is a swimming pool for spectators and competitors.
Contact: Donald R. Duncan, PO Box 245, Athena, OR 97813.
Portland Highland Games
Founded in 1952, the Games are currently held in the grounds of Mt Hood Community Centre on the third Saturday in July. They include a ladies frying pan toss, a pillow fight, and a sheepdog demonstration.

Contact: Dixie McKendrick, 4242 SW South Shore Blvd, Lake Oswego, OR 97034.

PENNSYLVANIA
Celtic Classic
Currently held in Bethlehem over the last weekend in September.
Contact: The Celtic Classic, 437 Main St, Suite 314, Bethlehem, PA 18018.
Delco Scottish Games
Founded in 1967, the Games are currently held on the third Saturday in June at Devon Horse Show Grounds. Attractions include a puppet show, fiddling and crafts demonstrations. Usually at least twenty pipe pipe bands attend. Grandstand seating is provided on both sides.
Contact: 181 Foxcatcher Lane, Medici, PA 19063.
Ligonier Highland Games
Founded in 1959 by Clinton F. Macdonald at Ligonier, some miles east of Pittsburgh, the Games are currently held on the first Saturday after Labor Day in Idlewild Park, a heavily wooded family amusement area. Attractions include pipe bands, solo piping, Highland dancing, heavy events and tug-of-war, also a sheepdog demonstration, Scottish fiddling and Celtic harp workshops as well as seven-a-side rugby.
Contact: David L.Peet, 359 Carlton Road, Bethel Park, PA 15102 *Tel*: (412) 831–1408.

SOUTH CAROLINA
Charleston Scottish Games and Highland Gathering
Charleston had the first St Andrew Society, founded in 1729. The Games, however, were only established in 1972 and are currently held on the third Saturday in September at Boone Hall Plantation in Mt Pleasant. A new world record of

thirty-one feet was set in the sheaf toss at the 1990 Games.

Contact: Scottish Society of Charleston, PO Box 10932, Charleston, SC 29411.

TENNESSEE
Great Smoky Mountains Gatlinburg Highland Games
Founded in 1985 and currently held over the third weekend in May, the Games include a women's kilted mile, haggis hurling, and a bonniest knees contest.

Contact: PO Box 84, Gatlinburg, TN 37738.

TEXAS
Dallas Scottish Highland Games
Founded in 1972 the Games are currently held on the first Saturday in September.

Contact: Robert C.Forbes, 8523 San Leanadro Drive, Dallas, TX 75218.

Houston Highland Games
Founded in 1967 the Games are generally held on the second Saturday in May in the grounds of St Thomas Episcopal School (with only 700 students the school has its own pipe band and Highland dancing is compulsory). The Games include a Viking raid on Scottish Highlanders, Morris dancers, clog hoppers and a sheepdog demonstration.

Contact: Houston Highland Games Association, PO Box 66, Bel Aire, TX 77401.

Texas Scottish Festival and Highland Games
These games are currently held in the Maverick Stadium, Arlington, on the first weekend in June.

Salado Highland Games
Founded in 1961 and currently held on the village green in a former stage-coach town during the second full weekend in November, these Games

attract a large attendance. They include sheep-dog trials.

Contact: Central Texas Area Museum Inc, Salado, TX 76571.

West Texas Highland Games

Founded in 1982 and organised by the Scottish Heritage Society, these small local Games are currently held on the second Saturday in October in the Garden and Arts Centre in Lubbock. They are preceded by a golf tournament.

Contact: PO Box 2081, Lubbock, TX 79408.

UTAH

Payson Scottish Festival

Founded in 1987 and currently held in the city park on the second Saturday in July. The Games are preceded by a golf tournament and include a women's frypan toss and Rolling-pin throw.

Contact: 300 South, Payson, UT 84651.

Utah Scottish Festival and Highland Games

Founded in 1974, the Games are usually held in mid-June in Jordan River Park in Salt Lake City. Events include women's stone throw, haggis hurling and a Scottish baking contest.

Contact: Utah Scottish Association, 483 8th Avenue, Salt Lake City, UT 84103.

VERMONT

Queechee Scottish Festival

Founded in 1972 the Festival is currently held on the third Saturday in August at Queechee Polo Field beside the river which bisects this small town. The Games include seven-a-side rugby, deerhound coursing, a ladies rolling-pin toss, an egg and spoon race, and a kilted mile.

Contact: Scotland-by-the-Yard, Queechee VT 05059.

Vermont International Highland Games

Founded in 1984 and presently held at Essex

Junction on the third Saturday in June. Attractions include clarsach playing and fiddling.
Contact: PO Box 692, Essex Junction, VT 05452.

VIRGINIA
Blue Ridge Highlands Scottish Festival
This Festival is currently held at the Victory Stadium, Roanoke in early September.
Tidewater Scottish Festival and Clan Gathering
Founded in 1979 and currently held in early June in Norfolk Botanical Gardens by the sea, where the International Festival of Roses is also held. Attractions include clan games, haggis hurl, Scottish dog breeds, and Scottish deerhound coursing.
Contact: Tidewater Scottish Festival, PO Box 2000, Virgina Beach, VA 23452.
Virginia Scottish Games
Founded in 1974 and usually held over the fourth weekend in July at the Episcopal High School in Alexandria, a town founded by Scots and now the sister city to Dundee. Although started comparatively recently, these have now become one of the major Games. They include celebrity haggis hurling, the US National Harp and Clarsach Championships, and Scottish deerhound coursing.
Contact: Virginia Scottish Games Association, Box 1338, Alexandria, VA 22313.
Williamsburg Scottish Festival
Founded in 1978 and held at the end of September on the Campus of the College of William and Mary (the second-oldest college in the USA, founded 1693). Attractions include a Scottish sheepdog demonstration. Competitors and Spectators can also visit the nearby historic area of Williamsburg.
Contact: Scottish Festival Inc, PO Box 866, Williamsburg, VA 23187.

WASHINGTON
Bellingham Highland Games
Founded in 1960 and currently held on the first
Saturday in June, the Games include pipe bands.
Contact: Isla Paterson, 639 Hunters Pt Drive,
Bellingham, WA 98225.
Pacific North-West Highland Games
Founded in 1945 and organised by the Seattle
Highland Games Association, these Games are
usually held in mid-August at the King County
Fairgrounds, Enumclaw and include a hay bale
toss.
Contact: Sharon Rirelis, 8802 Meridian Avenue,
N Seattle, WA 98103 *Tel*: 206 522 2874.
Spokane Scottish Festival and Tattoo
Founded in 1958 and currently held on the last
Saturday of July at Riverfront Park. The Games
include a keg toss and a tug-of-war.
Contact: Mary Alward, 418 E 11th St, Spokane,
WA 99202.
Tacoma Highland Games
Founded in 1968 and customarily held in mid-June
at Frontier Park, the Games are only open to resi-
dents from Washington, Oregon and Idaho.
Contact: Joyce Denton, 241 E 63rd St, Tacoma,
WA 98404.
Vashon Island Strawberry Festival and
Highland Games
Founded in 1984 and currently held on the
second Saturday in July. This small farming
community had celebrated its strawberry festi-
val for several years before local Scots added
the Games. They include a fiddling demonstration.
Contact: Sr Sterling Hill, 10450 15th Avenue,
SW Seattle, WA 98746.

WISCONSIN
Milwaukee Highland Games
Currently held at the beginning of June in Old
Heidelberg Park, Milwaukee.

EUROPE

DENMARK
St Andrew Society of Denmark
Founded 1949. Pres: Hamish I.B. Barclay, Kastelsvej
23, 2100, Copenhagen 0.

GERMANY
Caledonian Society of Hamburg
Founded 1966. Chief: P.L. Ogilvy-Stuart, Harveste-
huder, Weg 38, Hamburg.

SWEDEN
Stockholm Caledonian Dance Circle
Founded 1975. Pres: Anders Gorling, Aprikosgatan
31, S-162 36, Vallingby.

SOUTH AFRICA

**The Caledonian Society of Johannesburg and The
Federated Caledonian Society of Southern Africa**
The Caledonian Society of Johannesburg was
founded in 1891, when it held its first Highland Games. These continued until 1918/19 when
the various Caledonian Societies joined together
and formed the Federated Caledonian Society of
Southern Africa. This body then organised the
various Highland Games including the Johannesburg Gathering. Since 1932 the Annual Scottish
Gathering has been permitted to use the title Royal.
Today the Gatherings are mostly restricted to pipe
bands, Highland dancing and solo piping. The
traditional dates for the events are listed below,
but venues and dates are subject to alteration.

For details regarding all events contact: Charles Wilson, FSA Scot, Federation Secretary, The Federated Caledonian Society of Southern Africa, UCS Centre, 103 Simmonds Street, Braamfontein, Johannesburg, 2001 *or* PO Box 31424, Braamfontein, 2017 *Tel*: 9011) 403–1837.

Natal Scottish Gathering
First Saturday, April, Hoy Park, Durban.
Eastern Cape Gathering
Second Saturday, April, Port Elizabeth.
Irish Pipe Band Gathering
First Saturday, May, St John's College, Johannesburg.
Northern Johannesburg Caledonian Society Gathering
Third Saturday May, Guide Dog Training Centre, Johannesburg.
Natal South Coast Gathering
Last Saturday, May, Amanzimtoti.
Pretoria Caledonian Society
6 June, Christin Brothers College, Pretoria.
Southern Johannesburg Caledonian Society
16 June, St Martin's School, Rosettenville.
The Royal Scottish Gathering
First weekend September, Johannesburg.
Useful address
Caledonian Society of Pretoria
Founded 1892. Chief: S. Gibson, PO Box 971, Pretoria.

Critical Bibliography

The Athletes and Athletic Sports of Scotland, and J.W. McCombie Smith, FSA, Scot: A. Gardner, 1892.

> The first book to deal thoroughly with the Highland Games in Scotland. An interesting look at the Games as they were at the time, it notes the early presence of the 'strongest men in the world'.

'The Highland Games', E. Lennox Peel, in *The Encyclopedia of Sport*, E.Lennox Peel, Lawrence and Bullen, 1897.

> A short and rather patronising entry in a massive two-volume encyclopedia. No great originality apparent.

Shinty: A Short History of the Ancient Highland Game, Rev J. Ninian MacDonald, OSB, James Grant, 1932.

> A delightful attempt by a keen enthusiast to outline the history of the game. A pleasant small book.

Scottish Highland games, David Webster, Reprographia, 1973.

> The first author in this century to put down seriously the background and details of the Highland Games. Well illustrated with some good action pictures.

The Games, Charlie Allan, Famedrame, 1974.

> An attractive small book by one of the popular heavyweight contestants, giving details of the Games spiced with his own personal comments.

The Scottish Highland Games in America, Emily Ann Donaldson, Pelican Books, 1986.

With a foreword from David Webster this was the first book to illustrate the remarkable spread of the Highland Games throughout the USA in recent decades, well illustrated.

Camanachd: The Story of Shinty, Roger Hutchinson, Mainstream, 1989.

The definitive history of the game, well produced by the publishers, this is essential reading for anyone wishing to learn all about shinty.